Dancing with Change

Dancing with Change

A Spiritual Response to Changes in the Church

Dr. Richard J. McCorry

iUniverse, Inc.

New York   Lincoln   Shanghai

Dancing with Change
A Spiritual Response to Changes in the Church

iUniverse, Inc.

For information address:
iUniverse, Inc.
2021 Pine Lake Road, Suite 100
Lincoln, NE 68512
www.iuniverse.com

ISBN: 0-595-31462-7

Printed in the United States of America

TO MY MOTHER,

"THE WIND BENEATH MY WINGS"

In Christianity God is not a static thing—not even a person—
but a dynamic, pulsating activity, a life, almost a kind of drama.
Almost, if you will not think me irreverent, a kind of dance.

—C. S. Lewis
Mere Christianity

Contents

Introduction 1

    Importance of Developing a Spiritual Response to Change 3

    Scope and Limitations 3

    Summary 4

Chapter 1—Change 5

    Types of Change 6

    Stages of Change 6

    Psychology of Change: Resistance and Acceptance 8

    Consideration of Good Change vs. Bad Change vs. Inevitable Change 11

    Why Change is Necessary 12

Chapter 2—Change in a Religious Context 14

    Ways in Which Church Change/Reform Happens 16

    Factors That Retard Church Change 17

    Factors That Facilitate Church Change 17

Chapter 3—Theological Approach to Change 19

    Philosophical Underpinnings—The *I Ching* 19

    The Paschal Mystery and Change 24

    Theology of the Cross 27

Chapter 4—Spirituality During Times of Change 29

    Spirituality Is a Powerful Force for Change 30

    Essential Components of a Sustaining Spirituality During Times of Change 31

        Change in Scripture 31

            Hebrew Scripture 32

                Jeremiah as the Model Prophet for Spirituality During Times of Change 32

                Historical Context 33

                Admonitions 33

                Jeremiah's Fourfold Message 34

                    Judgment 34

                    Repentance 36

                    The Way of Obedience 37

                    Restoration 37

Christian Gospel 38
    How Jesus Personally Adapted to Change 38
    Change and Conflict in the Christian Scriptures 42
        Jesus and Conflict 42
        The Gentile Conflict in the Early Christian Community 44
Change in Tradition 50
    Church Councils 50
    Reformation Spirituality 51
Change in Sacraments 53
Chapter 5—A Spiritual Path Through Change—The LEAP of Faith 56
Introduction 56
Foundation 56
Elements 57
    Learning 57
    Experience 58
    Action 59
    Prayer 60
    Faith 62
Praxis 62
    Feedback 65
    One Person's Experience 65
Conclusion 69
Bibliography 71
About the Author 79

Acknowledgments

This book is an adaptation of my doctoral dissertation by the same title. This doctor of ministry degree in transformative leadership was conferred by Colgate Rochester Crozer Divinity School, in Rochester, N.Y. It was the considerable warmth and enthusiasm of those involved in the formation of the dissertation and the reviews of the finished product which encouraged me to take it to the next step and write this book.

The major danger one runs into while attempting to acknowledge all the people who have had a positive impact upon a book project such as this is forgetting someone. Fully cognizant of this danger, I humbly beg forgiveness from anyone I might inadvertently omit.

All glory, praise and honor belongs to our Lord Jesus Christ, for without Christ in my life this book could never have materialized. I need to thank especially, Fr. Douglas DellaPietra, a priest of the Roman Catholic Diocese of Rochester. Fr. Doug and I have worked side by side for the past four years, creating and delivering many of the "LEAP of Faith" reflection sessions, which are fully described in Chapter 5. It was his insights and support which helped to create much of the raw material from which this book was refined. I am most thankful, though, for his friendship.

I am deeply grateful to Dr. William Pickett, Director of Pastoral Planning for the Roman Catholic Diocese of Rochester, NY. For seven years, Dr. Pickett provided the "laboratory" in which much of the material for this book was created and refined. He also served as a member of my doctoral committee, providing guidance, support, and most importantly, his friendship. The mentor and chairperson of my doctoral committee, Dr. William Herzog II, Professor of New Testament at Colgate Rochester Crozer Divinity School, provided invaluable support and guidance throughout the writing of the dissertation. Dr. Stephanie Sauvé, Acting Dean of the Women and Gender Studies Program at Colgate Rochester Crozer Divinity School, the third cherished member of my doctoral committee, reminded me constantly of the importance of good cheer and taking care of self in ministry, valuable lessons which will pay dividends long after these pages have yellowed.

Dr. Anne Remmel, a change management consultant from Toronto, Ontario, Canada reviewed a draft of my dissertation, offered many constructive comments as well as guidance and emotional support during my dissertation defense. Mary Ann Fackelman and Ron Hein provided valuable editorial assistance during the final phases of writing my dissertation and this book.

Rev. Tim Niven, Rev. Michael Mayer, Rev. Norman Tanck, CSB, Rev. Peter Deckman, Rev. Bob Werth, Rev. Peter Clifford, Sr. Roberta Tierney, John Peltier, Karen Rinefierd, Mary Paul, Patricia Scouten and Casey Lopata served on an advisory committee and offered indispensable wisdom during the formative stages of the "LEAP of Faith" reflection sessions. Karen Rinefierd and Casey Lopata, Planning Group Liaisons for the Roman Catholic Diocese of Rochester, also encouraged many to attend the "LEAP of Faith" reflection sessions. Finally, I'd like to thank the many participants in the "LEAP of Faith" reflection sessions, for without their valuable and encouraging feedback this book might not have been written.

Introduction

Let's face it, change is difficult. And yet, change is our ever-present companion throughout this journey of life. John F. Kennedy, the thirty-fifth President of the United States, said, "The only unchangeable certainty is this, that nothing is unchangeable or certain."[1] Change comes in many forms. Seasons change. People are born and people die. We choose some changes and others are thrust upon us. Some changes are monumental and others are relatively easy to weather. Change has been a fact of life since before humans set foot on the planet, and due to many factors, not the least of which is the technological age in which we live, it appears that change is accelerating at breathtaking speed.

Imagine for a moment a large empty dance floor. As the music of life begins, change invites us to dance. As change leads, we follow, lest many missteps and stumbles arise along the way. The same is true of leaders, including Church[2] leaders: we all must first learn how to follow before we can lead. This is not to say that followers never lead change; however, leading change is beyond the scope of this inquiry, which reviews relevant spiritual means for adapting to changes in the Church.

Although change is inevitable, often our first reaction to change is opposition and fear and a refusal to dance. It would almost appear that we have some instinctive dislike for and an inherent resistance to change. This resistance to change is not always positive. What is it about the nature of change—including change in the Church—that causes us almost instinctively to rebel against it, to insist on marching or standing still when, in fact, we are invited to dance?

If we assume change in general is difficult, should we not expect that change within the Church is even more difficult? People often turn to the Church and their religion as the rock upon which they can stand amidst turbulent seas of change in the secular world. Often people from every tradition believe their religion is completely developed and fully revealed, to be passed on in exactly the same form that it was given to them. On the contrary, even a cursory reading of the history of most traditions proves the inaccuracy of this notion and shows that change has been a part of our Church since Christ's time and is certainly a reality today. Those who reminisce about an unchanging Church from their youth are

---

1. John F. Kennedy, *The State of the Union Address to Congress*, 1962.
2. All references to Church refer specifically to the Roman Catholic Church unless otherwise noted.

really entertaining the way they wish it could have been rather than reality. The truth is that just as in the rest of society, the only thing that is constant in Church history is change. The Church has always been called to reform itself, a call that many of the prophets both heralded and championed. Furthermore, the Church has needed to change in response to changes going on in the secular world. For the Roman Catholic Church during the last forty years, the pace of those changes has picked up and is increasing exponentially. For example, Vatican II "opened the windows" of the Church and began to allow the fresh air of modern relevance into an institutional culture mired in the Middle Ages. Change invited the Church to rise from its throne and to dance. The work of Vatican II is certainly far from complete, and in some cases is being actively undone. In addition, the decline in the number of priests has presented the sacramentally-based Church with the need to adapt to even more changes. At the very least, parishes and Mass schedules will need to be consolidated to accommodate fewer priests.

Since many seek refuge in the Church from the constant changes in the world around them, where can they turn when it is the Church that is changing, too? Some people operate out of their fear that change will adversely affect their faith life. Perhaps for some, it is simply a matter of comfort or routine. For many who are holding on to their faith by a delicate thread, because their Church appears to be a Church foreign to the one in which they grew up, the next seemingly minor change could cause their leaving for good. This is especially true if they see that change as moving away from God or, worse yet, as God moving away from them. What can the Church offer, by way of consolation and strength, to all those trying to cope with the changes in the Church?

Fortunately, those who seek ways of adapting to the changes occurring in the Church do not have to travel far. Our rich spiritual traditions, values and practices provide us with all that we need to adapt well to changes. It is, therefore, the purpose of this book to reveal, identify, and describe some of the spiritual tools that people can employ to adapt to the changes that are currently taking place in the Church. Ideally, this book will help us learn new spiritual dance steps.

Little is written specifically on the topic of a sustaining spiritually during times of religious and Church change. This book, therefore, reviews relevant spiritual means for adapting to changes in the Church from among the rich materials on spirituality. It also draws from contemporary psychology and secular change management and endeavors to distill a unique spiritual method for dealing with changes in the Church.

Importance of Developing a Spiritual Response to Change

The extent to which people can be helped to overcome their fear and ignorance of change in the Church will directly affect the life of faith communities in the midst of transition. Since significant changes are envisioned for the near and distant future, developing a spiritual response to these changes will hopefully have a positive impact upon the Church.

Additionally, spiritual tools designed to help people deal with changes in the Church could have implications for adapting to other types of changes that people constantly face. Since, as the Buddha is reported to have said, "Everything changes, nothing remains without change," a spiritual approach to changes in the Church could help all people of faith in the other changing areas of their lives.

Scope and Limitations

This book will identify some spiritual means by which people can cope with changes going on in the Roman Catholic Church, the tradition from which this writer emerges. While not specifically focused outside the Roman Catholic Church, it will illustrate that there is much from other Christian traditions, and in some cases beyond the Christian traditions, that can be employed to help us understand change in the Church.

It is hoped that many of these spiritual means will be ultimately identified; however, since spirituality is such a vast arena, it would be unrealistic to expect that all, or even a majority of spiritual approaches to change, will be identified and explored in this book. Although this book will not explore spiritual leadership in times of change, religious leaders, lay and ordained alike, need spiritual means for helping themselves adapt to changes in the Church before they can hope to lead others through changes. By employing the spiritual tools outlined in this book, it is hoped that Church leaders will be in a position to share with others the experience, strength, and hope they found by making use of these methods. Finally, while this work could have implications for dealing with many changes beyond religion and the Church, this book will be limited to helping people adapt to changes in the Church.

Summary

Since change is our ever-faithful dancing partner throughout life, and because change in the Church in particular often evokes anxiety and resistance, the identification of spiritual means for adapting to the inevitable is of great benefit. Hold this image of dancing with change in your mind as we consider and explore this topic throughout this book. Imagine others joining you and change on the dance floor, everyone dancing with his or her own version of change. Some dance well, some do not, some are wallflowers who refuse or are too afraid to dance. Yet, somehow, all are necessary, perhaps because we can learn much from everyone. Paying attention to the music (i.e., reading the signs of the times) gives us a hint, at least, as to what change will do next. Our goal then, and a considerable one at that, is to learn to dance gracefully and seemingly effortlessly with our ever-dependable partner, change.

Chapter 1—Change

What is change and what is there about the nature of change that makes so many of us resist it?[3] Since change and life are inseparable, it would seem that these are the first basic and important questions to tackle.

Change is simply a reality in today's fast-paced world. As James Champy and Nitin Nohria note in *Fast Forward*, "Change today is faster, more erratic, more elemental than ever before."[4] Evidence of this abounds.

In the business world:

- 45% of American companies have reduced their workforce every year since 1990.
- 85% of all businesses now out source services that were once performed in house.
- Merger and acquisition activity in business has risen steadily and has seen its all time high in the past decade.

Every day in America, in our fast-paced lives:

- 108,000 of us move to a different home.
- The United States Government issues fifty more pages of regulations.
- Americans purchase forty-five thousand new automobiles and trucks, and smash eighty-seven thousand of them.
- More than six thousand three hundred get divorced, while thirteen thousand get married.

And in our Churches:

- Fewer people regularly attend Church than just a decade ago.
- Eighty to eighty-five per cent of our Churches in America are on a plateau or are declining in terms of membership.

---

3.   Vince DiPiazza, "Please, No More 'Resistance to Change,'" *Public Management* no. 85 (Mar. 2003).

4.   James Champy and Nitin Nohria, *Fast Forward: The Best Ideas on Managing Business Change* (Boston: Harvard Business School Publication, 1996), xiii.

- The number of unchurched Americans escalated to sixty per cent or more in the 90s.
- Two-thirds of American children do not receive any religious training.[5]

The current pace of change is so far-reaching and rapid that closing our eyes to the course of events or indifferently ignoring them is not effective. With so many changes thrown at us, we can start to feel like victims of change or begin to resist change—especially if we do not have a say in the changes. On the other hand, when we embrace change by trying to foresee what is coming, we have more options.

Types of Change

Change comes in many forms. There is stifling, threatening change and alluring change. There is change for which we dreamt, and that which we dread. There are changes foisted upon us from without and there are the changes that come from our desires within. Recognizing the diverse range of change, this book focuses on the changes that need to occur within us so that we can respond positively to the changes that are occurring outside of us, specifically the changes in the Church.

Stages of Change

There are three major stages of adapting to change: simply put, the beginning, middle and end.[6] As is illustrated in Chapter 3, understanding these stages helps clarify change within the Catholic Church. According to Miller, the beginning of change always involves an ending (a good-bye). In order for the new to be, something must fall away. This part of change comes to us in different ways. Sometimes loss and the pain confront us first; at other times it is the beginning that confronts us first. In either case, we have to attend to something ending.

Our lives abound with various necessary and sometimes unnecessary deaths. There is the death of our youth, which is necessary for us to become adults. Some, however, choose not to let go of their youth. It is not that they are holding on to their optimism and playfulness, but that they have refused to grow up and accept

---

5. Michael F. Meister, *Challenged by Change: Perceptions and Perspectives* (Romeoville: Christian Brothers Publications, 1991), 23.

6. James Miller, *Nothing is Permanent Except* Change (Fort Wayne: Willowgreen, 1991), videotape.

the fact that they are growing older. Another death can be that of our wholeness, which happens when we suffer a grave physical and/or emotional trauma.

There is also the death of a dream. That dream might be the loss of the girl who chooses another. Perhaps it is the loss of that ideal job for which we are turned down. It can also be the death of a dream that we have for our children that is lost when they choose another path. Whatever form it takes, we all experience the death of a dream. To a certain extent we all are like the daughter of Jephthah the Gileadite (the young virgin girl whose father had promised to sacrifice her to God if he were successful in battle) in that we die unfulfilled (Jgs. 11:29-40).

There can also be the death of an idea we hold about God or the Church. The disciples on the road to Emmaus (Lk. 24:13-32) did not recognize Christ because they were too focused on the old Christ to recognize the new.

Like the death of dreams, we do not like goodbyes; they are painful. If a change is unwanted or unchosen, there is danger that the loss of what is ending can dominate our thinking to the exclusion of all else. On the other hand, if a change is desired and chosen, we may neglect endings, as if only the forthcoming change is important. This is not good because endings need our attention just as much as beginnings. We need to grieve in order to let go of the past, and denying our losses can lead to resentment or even magical thinking. The experience of Christ's disciples on Good Friday would be a good example of this stage of change.

According to Miller, there is also a middle to change. In this in-between stage there is an emptiness; we are no longer what we used to be, but we are not yet what we are going to become. This emptiness, however, can be a fertile emptiness, like the farmer's field right after the seed is planted. The field looks empty, but there is something beginning to happen just below the surface. This is a time of waiting—while deep undercover life is stirring.

Some define this as the time of transition, our inner adjustments to external changes. Alan Nelson, in *How to Change Your Church Without Killing It,* wrote that it is not the changes that kill us; it is the transitions.[7] The most dreaded stage or phase in the change process is the time of transition. The people of Israel complained most bitterly between Egypt and Canaan.

During the transition stage, chaos, confusion, insecurity and apprehension run rampant. In *Managing Transitions*, William Bridges lists other common emotions that occur during the transition process: anger, bargaining, anxiety, sadness, disorientation, and depression.[8] We may also feel unstable or uncertain, and our

---

7. Alan Nelson, *How to Change Your Church Without Killing It* (Nashville: West Publishing, 2000), 23.

8. William Bridges, *Managing Transitions: Making the Most of Change* (Reading: Addison-Wesley, 1991), 88-89.

stress level can increase. It is not simply a coincidence that these feelings resemble Kubler-Ross's stages of acceptance of death,[9] because with change, as stated earlier, we are experiencing a death of sorts.

The end of change is a new beginning. Beginnings sometimes arrive quietly and sometimes with a shout. In either case, if we have attended to our feelings in the previous two stages, we might even experience joy in this stage: joy at the newness of what has replaced the old. Beginnings are a way of life saying "yes." Alleluia, He is risen!

Psychology of Change: Resistance and Acceptance

Statistically, it is believed that 10% in any group will be early adapters to change, another 10% will never change no matter what, and 80% will be slow movers toward change.[10] Thus 90% of us will resist change at one point or another, and the 80% who are slow movers toward change will experience internal tension, torn between stability and openness to change, in a constant tug-of-war.

It is a peculiar characteristic of the human species to resist change, even though we are surrounded by tens of millions of other species that demonstrate wonderful capacities to grow, adapt, and change.[11] Likewise, we have ample evidence that species that fail to adapt become extinct. Nevertheless, we resist change. Why is that?

There is a host of reasons why people resist change, some more compelling than others. Every individual assesses how he/she will be affected by the change because every change can present both positive opportunities and dangerous negative outcomes. Whenever we encounter a new situation, our inherent response is to be on guard, physically and emotionally. Consider when we meet a new person. We commonly forget that person's name only seconds after we are introduced to them because our minds are busy processing all sorts of new information, such as evaluating the person's appearance and determining a category in which to put this person (friend or foe, trust or don't trust). This process can be exhausting which is why we gravitate toward routine and familiar people.

We typically struggle against change, seeing it as the source of disruption to our precious internal stability. Change can disrupt comfortable routines. It forces people to become conscious of, and to question, familiar routines and habits. People operating in unfamiliar territory use incredible amounts of emotional

9.   Elizabeth Kubler-Ross, *On Death and Dying* (New York: Macmillan, 1969), 64.

10. Steven Covey, *The Seven Habits of Highly Effective People* (New York: Simon and Schuster, 1989), 21.

11. Margaret J. Wheatley, *Leadership and the New Science: Discovering Order in a Chaotic World* (San Francisco: Berrett-Koehler Publishers, 1992), 138.

energy and easily become fatigued. Change removes predictability and stability, at least temporarily.

People may resist change because it requires them to give something up that they do not want to give up. Refusing to recognize the possibility of being downsized out of a job is but one example of resistance to change.

People often feel threatened by change because they sense that their identity is somehow being undermined.[12] For instance, when people closely identify with attending a particular church at a particular time each week, if the church or time is changed, on some level they may feel that their identity is being threatened. Consequently, they resist change that imperils their identity.

Conversely, one way to adapt effectively to change is to have a clear sense of our identity and to realize when this identity is being threatened.[13] This may require a person to dig beyond the many superficial identities we all have, to his or her core identity. For instance, instead of identifying oneself primarily as a person who attends St. Mary's Church every Sunday at 10 A.M., when one identifies oneself as a believer and follower of the Risen Lord, the person whose identity is that of a believer and follower does not have his or her identity threatened if the 10 A.M. Mass at St. Mary's is eliminated. Sadly, people have left the Church simply because their Mass time has been changed.

Another reason people resist change is because they feel that they have lost control. Unwanted change removes the illusion of control we have over our own lives. One method people use to reassert control is actively to resist the change that is causing them to feel that they have lost control. At the same time, though, cooperating with change and even becoming a change agent, can help one regain a sense of control even though the person might not have chosen the change in the first place.

People may also resist change because they are under stress that may not even be related to the impending change. Interestingly, psychologists have found that as our level of stress increases, our attention span diminishes. When this happens, people seek solutions to new problems in the same places where they found the old ones. In the face of stress and pressure, there is a measurable tendency to become rigid and resist new ideas.[14]

Change is resisted because people may fear an uncertain future. They battle against change out of fear of the future, rather than for love of the past. Others resist change out of revenge, as retaliation for past changes they did not choose or like.

12. Robert Kysar, *Stumbling in the Light: New Testament Images for a Changing Church* (St. Louis: Chalice Press, 1999), 35.

13. Ibid.

14. Robert Quinn, *Deep Change: Discovering the Leader Within* (San Francisco: Jossey-Bass, 1996), 54.

There are those who, when part of a group, have the best interest of the group at heart and honestly think it is a mistake to institute a change. These people may be wrong and instead of helping the organization, they end up damaging it. In other instances, people resist change because they are surprised: they did not see it coming. They may also resist change if they sense that there has been a lack of (or inappropriate) preparation for the change.

Self-doubt can cause people to resist change, particularly when they may have to perform differently under changed circumstances. They may doubt that they have the skills to operate in this new way. This is rarely expressed out loud, but nonetheless it can rob people of their self-confidence, which in turn promotes resistance to the change.

Uncertainty about where a change will take them or even what the next step will be or what it will feel like, can cause people to resist change. When people do not know where the change will take them, they dig in their heels. Further, resistance to change can occur if there is a perception of a forthcoming actual or imaginary loss of face. Another problem is that many people infer that accepting change means the way things were done in the past was wrong, which can be embarrassing for them, and some people will go to extreme lengths to save face.

People resist change because they believe the change will cause them to work harder or longer, and if change is perceived to require more energy, more time, greater mental preparation, or simply more work than they are willing to accept, it is resisted. Even "winners" can lose something in change because things will never be the same as they were before.

In addition, unresolved past grievances or gripes often fuel resistance to new ideas. This may be manifested in a conspiracy of silence or even malicious compliance, both forms of passive-aggressive behavior.

One reason many change initiatives are never implemented is because people have internal competing commitments. Kegan and Lehey, in their book, refer to this as our "hidden change immune system."[15] A person may be outwardly committed to a particular change but inwardly (even subconsciously) resist the change when the person thinks, for instance, that others will not like him or her if the change is implemented. Many of these competing commitments touch a narcissistic wound that most of us carry and of which most of us are not even aware. These narcissistic wounds[16] can unleash great energy toward resisting change.[17]

---

15. Robert Kegan and Lisa Lahey, *How the Way We Talk Can Change the Way We Work: Seven Languages for Transformation* (San Francisco: Jossey-Bass, 2001), 28.

16. The loss, fragmentation and lack of development of the core sense of self is the narcissistic wound.

17. Kegan, 135.

If people believe that the universe is on a relentless road toward death, and that death is the end, they cannot help but live in fear of change. In this downward spiraling world that they perceive, any change exhausts their store of valuable energy and leaves them empty, one step closer to death. They want to have nothing to do with change because, as they see it, only decline awaits them.[18]

People may also resist change when authority figures—or other people whose opinion they value—are opposed to the change. This is particularly operative when a first-line supervisor opposes a change and thereby influences all under her authority to do likewise.

Similarly, authority figures may oppose change if they perceive somehow that the change makes them look bad. This may be particularly true if they feel they have to have all the answers and, in fact, do not have answers for all the questions their subordinates may be asking them about an impending change.[19]

People will also resist change if their personal values are called into question; a change in attitudes and structures frequently calls accepted values into question. People working in telemarketing, for instance, may resist a change in their sales pitch if they perceive it to be unethical and beyond their personal compromise limits.

Consideration of Good Change vs. Bad Change vs. Inevitable Change

Change is not a monolith, and it can be categorized as "good" change, "bad" change, and "inevitable" change. Paul tells us in his second letter to the Corinthians that change can be good:

> And we all, with unveiled face, beholding the glory of the Lord, are
> being changed into his likeness from one degree of glory to another; for
> this comes from the Lord who is the Spirit (2 Cor. 3:18).

Sometimes good change is clear only with the passing of time, in much the same way as true prophecies are verified when they come true, even though large blocks of time may intervene.

In the *Decree on Ecumenism*, the Second Vatican Council stated unequivocally that the Church is in constant need of renewal.[20] Change is sometimes not only good; at times it is also necessary.

---

18. Wheatley, 77.
19. D. Mann, "Why Supervisors Resist Change & What You Can Do About It." *Journal for Quality & Participation* 23 (2000): 20.
20. Decree on Ecumenism, Vatican II, *Unitatis Redintegratio*, (21 Nov. 64), #5.

Whether or not a change is "bad" is also sometimes evident only with the passing of time. What can initially appear to be bad change, such as a divorce, can turn out with the passing of time to have been an occasion of great blessing, when the divorced person finds a truly holy marriage with another. Furthermore, bad change can sometimes be made good and holy by the way it is approached. Such was the case when a woman who had endured life in a concentration camp composed a prayer asking God to credit any suffering she might have endured as grace toward the forgiveness of her captors and tormentors.[21] The only bad change that can be discerned with certainty at the moment it happens is the change that entails giving up, such as abandoning the faith.

In the case of inevitable change, we may be unsure if it is good or bad; we know only that it is inevitable. Approached well, inevitable change provides an opportunity to turn "bad" change into "good" change. In many cases, it boils down to attitude, and attitude as Charles Swindoll wrote, is what matters most:

> The longer I live, the more I realize the impact of attitude on life...I am convinced that life is 10% what happens to me and 90% how I react to it. And so it is with you...We are in charge of our attitudes.[22]

There is some measure of irony in the fact that if we can adjust our attitudes about bad or inevitable change, we will see these changes in a new, more positive way. We also regain a certain amount of control over change by the positive attitude that we bring to it.

Why Change is Necessary

Change is necessary because it offsets our human tendency to want to fossilize our institutions. All active systems (a marital relationship, a sports team, the Church, or a business) must expand and grow, or they will contract and fall into a state of decay. To remain healthy and vibrant, a system must continuously evolve through the transformational cycle—routinization, desire, vision, experimentation, insight, confirmation, synergy, and mastery.[23]

Change is necessary in response to changing events or circumstances outside of us. In a commonplace example, if the grocery store at which we shop closes, we need to change where we get our groceries.

---

21. Joseph. Nassal, *Premeditated Mercy: Aa Spirituality of Reconciliation* (Leavenworth: Forest of Peace Books, 2000), 54.
22. Charles Swindoll, *The Grace Awakening* (Trenton: West Publishing, 2003).
23. Quinn, 168.

Individually, unless we have achieved sainthood status while still alive (as yet undone), every one of us needs a change of heart; we must set our gaze on the whole world and look to those tasks we can perform in order to bring about the betterment of the human race. Additionally, the most potent lever for changing others is modeling the change process ourselves.

Chapter 2—
Change in a Religious Context

A common admonition to new pastors is, "Do not make any changes for the first year." Some have even claimed that a pastor can preach outright heresy from the pulpit every Sunday and people will hardly notice. Have him move the furniture around and he will have armed insurgency!

Evidence of change and its effects in the Church today abounds, both positive and negative. For example, 80% of professional, paid, lay ministers are women who are performing many of the tasks reserved to priests just a short forty years ago. Further, while hard to quantify, there is an increasing sense of institutional stress borne of fear, which manifests itself by an increasing polarity around particular issues. The late Cardinal Bernadin's *Common Ground* initiative was intended to address this emergence of polarity. It is not without a certain measure of irony that *Common Ground* has itself become a polarizing issue. Those who are certain that they are the sole possessors of the "truth" of the Catholic faith see no need to try to find common ground with the others, while the others ask, "What harm can come from discussion?"

There is increasing trans-national consciousness and recognition of our global economic interdependency. Philip Jenkins in *The Next Christendom: The Coming of Global Christianity* asserts that in most of the major world religions there is a rise of reactionary fundamentalism, which is in response to the negative changes they see happening in our world generally and in their religion particularly.[24]

Sometime in the past forty years or so, there has been for many, in the U.S. at least, a disconnect between spirituality and religion.[25] This can be evaluated both positively and negatively. On the one hand, this disconnect has happened because organized religion has disappointed people. On the other hand, this is evidence that people are still searching for their connection to God and ways to bring meaning to the human condition.[26] One down side to this search for a spirituality apart

---

24. Philip Jenkins, *The Next Christendom: The Coming of Global Christianity*. (Oxford: Oxford University Press, March 2002), 231.

25. William L. Portier, "Spirituality in America : Selected Sources," *Horizons* 23, Spr 1996, p 140-161. Cf. David J. Tacey, *Remaking Men: Jung, Spirituality and Social Change* (New York: Routledge, 1997), 111.

26. Jenkins, 231.

from religion is that it can lead to "feel good religion," demonstrated by those ascribing to the "health and wealth" gospel today.

Currently in the U.S. Catholic Church, there are several factors driving Church change: suburbanization of the faithful, decline in the number of clergy and those choosing religious life, dwindling numbers of Catholics sending their children to Catholic schools, and the clergy sex abuse scandals.

Despite all the changes occurring in the Church, the Church is still seen by many as the sure refuge in times of change. No matter how crazy with change the secular world becomes, the Church is regarded as the place of solace. In the past, religion has functioned as society's glue, reminding people who they are and slowing down the rate of change—an oasis of peace in the midst of conflict and change. Many view religion as basically conservative and believe on some level that it should not be changed or adjusted. Reform in the Church is difficult because it is almost the nature of this institution to resist change.

So, where do people go for refuge when it is the Church that is changing along with the rest of the world? Perhaps a more apt question might be: Is our image of an unchanging Church real, or merely a creation of our own imagination?

> Religion is never a finished product, packaged, delivered, and passed intact from generation to generation. There are some in every religious tradition who think of their religion that way, insisting it is all contained in the sacred texts, doctrines, and rituals they themselves know and cherish. But even the most modest journey through history proves them wrong.[27]

In the religious establishment, changes have often begun as heresies. A good Christian example of this is Jesus Christ. Scribes and Pharisees often rent their garment(s) over something Jesus said or did. He was labeled a blasphemer and a heretic by the established religious authorities of his day. Additionally, many of the writers of Vatican II documents were considered outside the mainstream, some even "persona non grata," before the opening of this recent Church Council.

An examination of our religious heritage will also reveal a spirit of creative protest and prophetic criticism of the institutional Church. There is a great need for the Church to re-examine itself constantly in light of God's self-revelation in Jesus Christ to keep us on the right path.[28] Without change in the Church, we

---

27. Diana Eck, *A New Religious America: How a Christian Country Has Become the World's Most Religiously Diverse Nation* (Chicago: Erlbaum Associates, 2002), 9.

28. Alister E. McGrath, *Spirituality in an Age of Change: Rediscovering the Spirit of the Reformers* (Grand Rapids: Zondervan, 1994), 27.

are constantly pulled in the direction of deifying our buildings, our practices, and even our ministers. As Robert Carroll observes, "The past is never an exhaustive norm for the present unless one believes in a static God or frozen history."[29] In fact, Christianity is all about change: the personal call to conversion, repentance, and holiness.

Ways in Which Church Change/Reform Happens

Although resistant to change, religious traditions do reform themselves in various ways, sometimes for the better and sometimes for the worse. Sometimes these changes come from the top down, from the governing body of the institution (such as when the Southern Baptist Conference ruled that women could no longer be senior pastors in their Churches.) Likewise, in 2002 the United States Conference of Catholic Bishops issued a document approving, under limited circumstances, people other than priests preaching in the Churches.

Sometimes massive societal movements outside the Church influence the Church to reform itself. These societal movements are not necessarily organized and may occur spontaneously. For instance, in the early Church the charging of interest for a loan was banned. Nevertheless, society essentially ignored this ban and eventually the Church's opposition to this practice disappeared.

Governments have changed Churches. Some would hold that the greatest disaster to befall the Christian Church was when Constantine pronounced Christianity as the state religion for the Roman Empire. The impact that this pronouncement had upon the Church can be read in history. A more contemporary example of a government changing a Church occurred when Utah was being considered for statehood. In order for the Congress to ratify Utah's statehood, the Mormon Church had to agree to forego its practice of polygamy.

Finally, it is the "voice of the people" that can bring about change. Although at least once yearly confessions are still a requirement of the Church, known by some as the "Easter duty," there has been a precipitous decline in private confessions. People essentially are "voting with their feet."

Currently, the Catholic Church finds itself in the midst of a massive social movement that may ultimately cause it to change one of its stances. The Catholic Church has forever banned the use of birth control, even reaffirming that ban in 1979 with the release of the papal encyclical entitled *Humane Vitae*. Nevertheless, study after study has shown that Catholics practice birth control without compunction.

---

29. Robert P. Carroll, *From Chaos to Covenant: Prophecy in the Book of Jeremiah* (New York: Crossroad, 1981), 276.

Finally, on occasion a charismatic leader will come along and change the Church. Augustine and Luther, for instance, have both left their mark at turning points in Church history.

Factors That Retard Church Change

Change-weary people view Churches as bastions of relief. They muse that in this world of constant change it is nice to know there is one place that stays the same: the Church. Although evidence of changes in the Church abounds, at the same time it is clear that the Church changes more slowly than other organizations. This is due to several factors.

Many of those in Church leadership see themselves as tradition keepers, pre-servers of the past. They see as their duty perpetuating the values of the historical Church, such as Scripture teaching and maintaining time-tested doctrines.

Culture also plays a large role in the way Churches operate. In our current cul-ture, for instance, in order to avoid hurting feelings and damaging relationships, many tend to avoid issues that can create conflict. Creative approaches to conflict, however, are the oil which lubricates the mechanisms of change; the absence or sti-fling of conflict tends to retard the change process and make it more explosive when it does happen. We will consider the interplay of change and conflict more fully later in Chapter Four.

Factors That Facilitate Church Change

Coexistent with the factors that retard Church change, there are several aspects of the Church that can cause it to change more efficiently than other organizations. The primary reason is that the Church is under the guidance and support of the Holy Spirit. It is that same Holy Spirit who brought about changes during Jesus' time and, for that matter, throughout history. The Spirit was hovering over the chaos in Genesis just as the Spirit hovers over the seemingly chaotic changes of today.

Our goal, as Catholics, should be to bring about the Kingdom of God here on Earth. As we meditate upon the various parables Jesus told to describe the Kingdom of God and compare these images with the world around us, it is clear that there are many necessary changes ahead for us. Consider, for example, the parable of the generous landowner. In this story, the landowner pays the workers in his field the same amount, whether they worked twelve hours, six hours, or three hours. This sense of fairness is quite different from the world's sense of fair-ness and demonstrates how much we have yet to change. It is not only the world;

it is as obvious that the Church needs to undergo changes until it truly represents the kingdom of God here on Earth. The power of our call and our passion to fulfill it should make us more open to change in order to see God's work completed.

Generally speaking, family sticks together, certainly more so than perfect strangers. Because Churches emphasize the importance of relationships and tend to function somewhat like a family, they also tend to be more resilient in the face of internal and external stress.

The sacramental structure of the Catholic Church is designed to provide grace during times of change. The sacrament of matrimony, for instance, provides grace to people as they transition from the single to the married life. The role of sacraments during times of change will be discussed more fully in Chapter Four.

Finally, our history and higher calling prepare us for change. Our history is full of stories where God moved the people into promised lands and created fresh ministry opportunities for them. From the moment that Sarah and Abraham left the land of Ur to the present time, the history of our Church is an account of constant change. In every generation, the people of God have found a spiritual grounding that has sustained them throughout all the changes they faced.

Chapter 3—
Theological Approach to Change

Our spirituality emerges from our theology, our concept of God and our relationship with God. Theology can be attributed to some organized cult, such as Christian theology, or it can be of our own creation. The theologies that most of us embrace are largely a combination of the two. Here we will examine one theological variant which can inform our quest for a spirituality that will sustain us during times of change in the Church.

Philosophical Underpinnings—The *I Ching*

We construct our theology through the lens of a particular philosophy. Most historical forms of Christian theology rely upon Greek philosophy for providing the lens through which we consider God and the significance of God's son, Jesus Christ.

It is in the domain of Greek philosophy that we find a proclivity toward exclusive dualisms and absolute categories. For instance, observing that we are mutable creatures and believing that God, unlike ourselves, is perfect in every way, has led Christian theologians throughout the ages to conclude that God must be unchanging. Is it any wonder, then, that change has been vilified in religious circles, based upon this philosophy? Since God is supposedly all good and unchangeable, it would logically follow that those things that change are automatically bad in some fashion. Taking this to an extreme, in the early 1800s, Cardinal Newman wrote a treaties on the unchangeability of dogma, which applied very tortured logic and reasoning since it is clear that dogma has changed over time.[30]

Nevertheless, this particular way of thinking has provided a schema by which we can gain some insights into the unknowable, a God capable of creating such a wondrous universe and beings as complex as ourselves. At the same time, however, the exclusive dualistic categories of Greek philosophy present us with as many problems as they attempt to solve. For example, believing that our faith is the "true" faith has caused many to conclude that any other faith must be false. This tendency toward Christian exclusivity grows out of, in part at least, its

---

30. Cardinal J. H. Newman, *An Essay on the Development of Doctrine* (London: Longmans, 1845).

dependence upon Greek dualistic philosophy with its limiting categories. Consequently, in the past, Christians had little interest in dialogue with or even accommodation of other faith traditions; instead the goal was simply to take them over and convert their followers. Not only is this a negative history for our Church; it is not even consistent with the original messages of both the Jewish and Christian faiths.

The Jewish people, for example, were to extend hospitality to all according to the Torah: Jew and Gentile alike. Building upon this, Christ left the Church with the great command to love our neighbor as ourselves (Mt. 19:19). Yet, just like the Pharisees of Christ's day, many Christian theologians, past and present, have drawn a tight circle around the Church, declaring those inside the circle the elect and those outside the circle the damned.

Further, one might ask: who is to say that God cannot change? We believe that all things are possible with God, that God is omnipotent. It would appear that once we claim that God cannot change, we are limiting God's abilities. If God is truly unchangeable, how do we account for God's apparent change of mind in Scripture, such as when Abraham bargained with God to save Sodom for the sake of ten righteous persons (Gn. 18:23-32)?

Consider further where Greek philosophy takes us as we ponder the issue of suffering. Since historical Christian theology holds that God is an unchangeable being, it is impossible for God to feel since this would require some change to occur. Yet Christian preachers throughout the ages have proclaimed to the world that God is compassionate. Since compassion means "to feel with," how can this be, since God cannot feel? This is but one example of how far from our original faith tradition Greek philosophical thinking can take us.[31]

So, when it comes to change, what can we learn from a God who Greek philosophy has declared, never changes? Very little, it would seem, and this presents us with a conundrum.

No such dilemma exists, however, for students and followers of eastern philosophy, particularly the Chinese. One of the oldest books from Chinese antiquity, dating back to at least 200 B.C.E., is the *I Ching*, translated as: the book of changes. Here change is described as the constant, ongoing process of production and reproduction. Change is never ending, according to the *I Ching*; in fact, change is the ultimate reality.[32] Since God, too, is the ultimate reality, the Chinese have no difficulty conceiving of a God who is constantly changing and yet changeless at the same time.

---

31.   Jung Young Lee, *The Theology of Change: A Christian Concept of God in an Eastern Perspective* (Maryknoll: Orbis, 1979), 125-6.

32.   Ibid., 3.

This Chinese philosophy is characterized by inclusive dualisms symbolized by the yin and the yang, the great light and the great darkness, the sun and the moon, the creative and the receptive, just to name a few of the many names given to these characters. They are not exclusive dualities, since each is seen as complementing the other. Neither can exist without the other. They are divided and united at the same time. Any distinctions between them are conditional and existential, but not essential.[33] Yin becomes yang by union, while yang becomes yin by separation. Yin expands, while yang contracts. In these two figures, the Chinese find represented the entire mechanism of change.[34]

According to Lee, the Chinese see the "whole process of change as both independent and complementary."[35] Similarly, Rosemary Haughton in *Images for Change* observes that the relationship between continuity and change is not that of opposites, but is complementary.[36]

Viewing God through this philosophical lens, there is no problem conceiving of a God who feels with us, a much more comforting concept than the unfeeling God Greek philosophy requires, and one that harmonizes much better with the God revealed in both testaments.[37]

Is it acceptable, though, to apply the *I Ching* to construct a Christian theology? It would seem to be so, since the *I Ching* is not an eastern theology but simply an eastern philosophical way of thinking. Using the wisdom it can provide is no different than our two-millennium long tradition of viewing Christian theology through the Greek philosophical lens.[38]

Change is the basic ingredient for eastern thought. God is both being and becoming.[39] In a theology of change, based upon the Chinese philosophy specified in the *I Ching*, change is the source of becoming, which is the reality of being.[40] The logic supporting the theology of change is inclusive, both/and, as well as this/that. When we read in Scripture of the changelessness of God (Mal. 3:6, Ps. 102:26-7, Heb. 13:8), it means that God is constantly changing. The part of God that remains changeless is the fact that God is constantly changing.[41]

---

33. Lee, 3-6.
34. Ibid.
35. Ibid., 8.
36. Rosemary Haughton, *Images for Change: The Transformation of Society* (New York: Paulist Press, 1997), 2.
37. Lee, 125-6.
38. Ibid., 26.
39. Ibid., 19.
40. Ibid., 120.
41. Ibid., 43.

Thus, paradoxically, change never changes. The concept of a Creator God necessitates change. Clearly, when God created heaven and Earth, something in God's existence changed.[42]

Sin is the existential estrangement of the creature from the creator.[43] In this change theology, one longing for the past and exhibiting an inherent unwillingness to change manifests sinfulness. Of course, this resistance to change needs to be distinguished from those who resist change out of good conscience. The resistance to change being described here is resistance for the sake of resistance, unaccompanied by honest reflection and courageous discernment. Augustine's concept of original sin could be understood as our innate human tendency to resist change. The idea of a free will is our ability to cooperate or not cooperate, as we choose, with God's plan of change for the world. We, therefore, are both free and not free at the same time, because of the interplay between the concepts of free will and sin.[44]

A life of sin, manifested by resistance to change, is a life of suffering, since change continues while the sinner is out of alignment with the process.[45] Put another way, sin is a disruption of the change process, interfering with its normal functioning.[46] Sin is a reflection of humanity's desire to "be," that is to replace God, rather than to "become."[47]

Overcoming this resistance to change and being restored to God's work of creativity is another view of salvation. When Jesus said, "I am the way," (Jn. 14:6) He meant the way of change. When Jesus told his disciple to "follow me, and leave the dead to bury the dead" (Mt. 8:22), He meant, do not look back but only forward. Stay out of the past and move on to a changing future. To be in Christ, that is to be changing, requires that we give up our fruitless attempts at finding security by trying to establish our being in the past.[48]

Christ is the yang; we are the yin. The only proper response for our yin is to respond to Christ's yang. This response must include letting go of the past. Jesus told us, "He who would save his *[past]* life will lose it, but he that loses his *[past]* life for my sake shall have everlasting life." (Mt. 16:25, *[italics]* added to illustrate the point). By letting go of the past, we become one with the way of change: Christ's way, the way of salvation.[49]

---

42. Lee, 67.

43. Ibid., 92.

44. Ibid., 122.

45. Ibid., 92-3.

46. Ibid., 93.

47. Ibid.

48. Ibid.

49. Ibid., 95.

Salvation then, is harmony between change and changing, the creature and the creator.[50] Does God intend for us to change? Look at the facts: we are constantly changing from the moment of our conception to the moment of our death and beyond. There is no moment in our lives when we are exactly the same as in the previous or next moment. That is how we are built; change is the reality of our existence. When we claim "to be saved, it means that we are in accord with the principle of change."[51]

Christ the Savior, then, is at the center of God's creative process.[52] "I am the alpha and the omega, the beginning and the end" (Rev. 22:13). He is the symbol for perfect change.[53]

Rosemary Haughton points out in her book *Images for Change* that, "Theology has always been the expression, caught in one moment of time, of an ever changing movement of thinking, feeling and experimenting."[54] Likewise, Ronald Preston observed in his article "Reflections on Theologies of Social Change," that, "[We] need to work at theologies which have a built-in ability to cope with change, and which fortify people in the arduous task of making constructive use of the changes which will be going on in our world anyway."[55] At this moment in time, where change is the common denominator of so much of our reality, the theology of change, as Lee has coined and defined this concept, informs our quest for a spirituality which will sustain us during times of change in the Church.

Consistent with this theology of change, a worthy goal for a spirituality during times of change in the Church would be to maintain the best of the tradition while still changing with the times.[56] It can no longer be either/or; it is now both/and. The spirituality of change should interweave continuity and change, maintaining our foundation while practicing flexibility.

---

50. Lee, 95.

51. Ibid., 95.

52. Ibid., 97.

53. Ibid.

54. Haughton, 175.

55. Ronald H. Preston, "Reflections on Theologies of Social Change." In *Theology and Change: Essays in Memory of Alan Richardson* (London: S C M Press, 1975), 164.

56. Leighton Ford, *Transforming Leadership: Jesus' Way of Creating Vision, Shaping Values and Empowering Change* (Downers Grove: InterVarsity Press, 1993), 277.

The Paschal Mystery and Change

The Paschal Mystery is at the heart of Christianity. It is Christ's death leading to his rising to a new life and leaving his spirit among us. It has become axiomatic for the Christian's life, as Paul observed, "For if we have been united with him in a death like his, we shall certainly be united with him in a resurrection like his" (Rom. 6:5). Christ's crucifixion and resurrection, therefore, can be one lens through which to view all the changes we encounter in the Church.[57]

Christ's disciples experienced the Paschal Mystery over the three days we now know as Good Friday, Holy Saturday and Easter Sunday. These three days provide us with a framework within which we can consider the stages of change and our positive response to them. Revisiting the three stages of change introduced in Chapter One will help us better understand change within the context of the Catholic Church.

Every change begins with an ending. Something must come to an end before something new can come about. Here we begin the journey of giving up and letting go; giving up what was, to gain what is yet to come. Jesus first had to die on Good Friday before he could rise on Easter Sunday. Likewise, every change involves a death of sorts. Sometimes it is a little death, such as moving away from the home in which we grew up. Sometimes it is a larger death, such as the actual death of a loved one or the ending of a significant relationship in our life.

The Paschal Mystery question for us is, "How do we regain new life and spirit after suffering one of life's many deaths?" First we need to consider the nature of death. Without the Paschal Mystery, death is terminal; everything is over, there are no new possibilities. Death, in light of the Paschal Mystery, is that which leads to new life and renewed possibilities.[58]

Before any significant change can take place within the Church, we must start a period of releasing, of burying the dead, of mourning their loss, of celebrating the cherished memories. In order for a fruitful change to occur, we must allow the death of something else.[59]

Grieving a death involves some measure of suffering. Suffering for suffering's sake alone has no value. Suffering in light of the Paschal Mystery can lead to life: life on the other side of suffering. Suffering makes us vulnerable and open to receiving love. Suffering leads us to our limits. To enter into suffering is to walk

---

57. Ford, 100.
58. Ronald Rolheiser, *The Holy Longing: The Search for a Christian Spirituality* (New York: Doubleday, 1999), 146.
59. Nelson, 65.

upon holy ground, for it is upon this ground that God lets us know how deeply we are loved.[60]

In the video *Nothing is Permanent Except Change*, Dr. James Miller offers some practical advice for what we must do in this beginning stage of change.[61] Most importantly, we must feel our loss. We must consider other losses we have experienced and appraise our past patterns of dealing with loss. We may find, by doing this, that there is a past loss that is connected in some way with the current loss.

We will experience a host of feelings during this phase. The best way out of this stage is to go through it. We need to honor the feelings that come naturally during this stage. Doing so will leave us much better prepared to accept what is ahead. We need to trust the process of experiencing these feelings; they are normal and natural. At the same time, we need to be on guard so that we do not get stuck in our feelings. Anger, for instance, is a common feeling when we are experiencing an ending. Anger sometimes makes us feel powerful and in control, especially when imposed change has us feeling out of control. It is easy to get stuck in anger as long as we are feeling out of control.

We need to assess realistically what is ending. As was discussed in Chapter One, relative to resistance to/acceptance of change, we need to identify our core, and determine how much this change is or is not affecting our core. What are we choosing to let go of and what are we choosing to embrace? In the same way that the resurrected Christ told Mary Magdala not to cling to Him (Jn. 20:11-18), we must refuse to cling to the past.

It is helpful if we mark our endings and remember them in some fashion. We can do this in a variety of ways: talking with an understanding friend or loved one, journaling our remembrances and the feeling of letting go, and/or ritualizing our loss in some way.

The middle stage of change can be compared to the Holy Saturday experience for the disciples. We can never fully appreciate what Holy Saturday must have felt like for the disciples because we know the rest of the story. The disciples did not have a clue about what was to come the next day, even though Jesus had alluded to the resurrection several times. They had given up everything: friends, family, home, and career, in order to follow this man whom they loved and believed was the anointed one. The disciples had watched Him die a criminal's death, die like a mere mortal and not like the Messiah they had thought Him to be. Well, now what? What was to become of the rest of their lives? Imagine all the emotions that must have welled up inside the disciples; that would be a taste of what this middle stage of change is like.

---

60. Patricia H. Livingston, *Lessons of the Heart: Celebrating the Rhythms of Life.* (Notre Dame: Ave Maria Press, 1992), 80.
61. Miller, Videotape.

There was great uncertainty among the disciples about the future. The disciples must have felt an emptiness, but it was an emptiness we can now describe as a fertile emptiness. When we experience change in the Church, this emptiness can be manifested as a spiritual hunger of sorts. Many have described spiritual hunger as the hole in the middle of our soul. It is that hole we try to fill with all kinds of earthly stuff (food, buying, sex, drugs, alcohol, risk, people), but it is a hole that can be filled only by the infinite.[62] St. Augustine said it best: "Our hearts are restless until they rest in thee."[63]

In spite of the fact that spiritual hunger is unsettling and painful, properly approached it can bring about blessings, that is, growth in the spirit. Just like Jesus' temptation in the desert helped Jesus realize his identity with the Father, deprivation helps us realize that God is the only true source of our identity.

Fear and an unwillingness to claim spiritual hunger blocks our ability to grow in faith and claim the change that lies before us. Spiritual hunger is the gift of being finite, because it creates a place for, and connects us to, the infinite—if we allow it. We believe that God wishes desperately to fill that hole in order to make us whole! No stone is left unturned by God in the quest to fill that hole in us. God moves mountains, sends us countless messengers, leads us to "green pastures and beside still waters" in order to fill us. God patiently waits, never giving up hope, never tiring of our own fruitless attempts to fill the hole ourselves, behind all the barriers we erect, ever vigilant for that time of our vulnerability when in desperation we will finally reach out to God, pleading for the solution to filling this hole. "Blessed are they who hunger," said the Lord, "for they will be satisfied" (Mt. 5:6).[64]

Times of difficulty are important and necessary because they remind us that we are not in charge and that we must turn to the One who is in charge. They remind us of how vulnerable and fragile we really are, despite the tough exterior we might try to maintain. The strong feelings we have around change, even seemingly innocuous changes, can cause some to leave a Church and abandon a faith they have practiced for many years.

In this middle stage of change we must work toward shifting our perspective. The biblical story of David and Goliath provides an apt example. David did not say, "Wow, he is so big, how can I ever defeat him?" He said, "Wow, he is so big, how could I ever miss him?"[65] This shift in perspective does not come naturally, and so we need to work on it.

---

62. Rolheiser, 115.
63. St. Augustine, *The Confessions of St. Augustine* (New York : Fordham University Press, 1989), 213.
64. Rolheiser, 115.
65. Livingston, 90.

In the middle stage of change we need to nurture hope. For with hope, there must be God. We need not be fixated on every disappointment or intensify every worry. Instead, we need to remember the times when, although it seemed unlikely, we made it through. This requires work because our natural tendency is often to focus on the negative. Ignoring hope is like ignoring love; eventually it will go away.[66]

In *Lessons of the Heart*, Patricia Livingston offers a prescription for hope.[67] We must be aware of and avoid feelings of dread. We need to place ourselves in the presence of beauty, in whatever form that might be for us: taking in a play, listening to music, reading a good book, or experiencing humor. Recalling instances of victory rather than defeat, will nurture God's spirit of hope within us.

The end of change is a new beginning, the Easter morning experience. "Alleluia, He is Risen!" We have let go of the old; new life, resurrected life is upon us. Sometimes we get quite comfortable and learn how to survive in the hunger, but we also need to recognize and enjoy the feast when it presents itself. We need to be able to reach out and embrace all the joy we can in those fleeting moments of feast when they present themselves (for example, when your twenty-year-old son sends you an e-mail saying that you are the best father he could have asked for!)[68] We must revel in those moments when we feel that true spiritual connection with God and revisit those moments often when we are in the desolation of subsequent Good Friday and Holy Saturday experiences. This is what builds hope for us in the future.

The Paschal Mystery is not complete without the Ascension, Pentecost and the gift of the Holy Spirit. The Ascension reminds us that the process of letting go of the old does not end with Good Friday, but takes some time to process. Pentecost reminds us of the importance of having a renewed spirit in order to live the new life of change.[69]

Theology of the Cross

"Take me to the cross, pastor," is an often heard refrain during sermons in the Black Church tradition. For some, the only theology they need is the theology of the cross. This can also inform our search for a spirituality that sustains us during times of change in the Church.

---

66. Livingston, 91.
67. Ibid., 115.
68. A great blessing which this writer recently received.
69. Rolheiser, 149.

The cross of Christ challenges our attempts to understand God through common sense because why would God choose to be revealed in this way? The cross rejects human reason. Likewise, many times in the early stages of change, our reason hinders us in our attempt to see God's purpose in this change. With an Easter morning perspective, which can come only by grace and the passage of time, we can discern God's hand at work.

The cross of Christ challenges experience as a source of authority. Experience needs interpretation and critique. For observers of the crucifixion, the experience was that God was absent. At one point, even Christ experienced God as absent. The resurrection, however, proved that was not the case. This is a good source of consolation for those suffering and feeling that God is absent from their struggle to adapt to changes in the Church.[70]

The cross reminds us that suffering is a part of being Christian. Any notion that being Christian is without effort was repudiated by the cross. Christian spirituality, born of the cross, requires that we work our way through suffering to reach the new life on the other side. Suffering and faith are intimately linked by the cross.[71] The theology of the cross rejects our temptation to create a self-centered "what is in it for me?" spirituality. The cross is a sign of hope that, no matter how difficult the change might be to deal with, love prevails in the end.

---

70. McGrath, 83.
71. Ibid., 87.

Chapter 4—
Spirituality During Times of Change

Defining spirituality is a bit like trying to define a particular tree. Certainly the tree exists and is subject to description, and yet there could be as many descriptions as there were people looking at the tree.

The English word "spirit" comes from the Latin "spirare," meaning "breath." Spirit can therefore be understood as a poetic name for the animating force in living beings. Spirituality then is a quality animating life.

We all have a spirituality. It is what we do with the fire that burns within us.[72] Both Charles Manson and Mother Theresa had a personal spirituality, though we would give little for that of the former and find that of the latter priceless.

A good friend, Fr. Bob Werth, defines spirituality quite simply: "It is the way we handle the human condition." In this attempt to define the scope and content of spirituality, it is helpful to refer to the question posed by Urban Holmes in *A History of Christian Spirituality:* "How does a Christian understand what it is to seek God and to know [God]?"[73] The ultimate spiritual question for a Christian is what does it mean to be a Christian and what is the relationship between my faith and the way I live my life?[74] Refining this question into the particular context of this book, our quest is to understand how a Christian can seek God and know God in times when our earthly reference point to God, the Church, is changing in small and not so small ways. This knowledge of God is highly transformative, capable of changing the mental, experiential, and even social worlds of those who grasp it.[75]

Popular spirituality, in the Roman Catholic tradition, used to be understood as duties and practices such as rosaries, devotions, visits to the Blessed Sacrament, attending Mass, meditation, and reading spiritual material.[76] Contemporary notions of spirituality view it as a way of relating to God in the everyday moments of our lives. Spirituality involves being receptive to all

---

72. Rolheiser, 6.
73. Urban T. Holmes, *A History of Christian Spirituality, An Analytical Introduction* (New York: The Seabury Press, 1980), p. 3.
74. Ibid. 28.
75. McGrath, 23.
76. Livingston, 33.

the little ways that God is revealed in the ordinariness of life. It is letting go and trusting that with God all things work for the good. Spirituality, therefore, is not set apart from life; it is how we respond to life. We can meet God when gifts are given to us and we can meet God when those things are taken away.[77]

One of the problems with the term spirituality is that for some it has the meaning of the interior as opposed to the exterior life and therefore is not connected exactly with the way we live. Spirituality, however, is lived; it is not just practices, principles and ideals. It is the way ideals are made visible in the way people live their lives. Spirituality is at the crossroads of theology and human existence.[78] Spirituality with any depth must struggle with the issue of suffering and death.[79] Since every change involves at least a little death, a spirituality that sustains us during times of change must likewise deal with the issues of suffering and death.

Spirituality Is a Powerful Force for Change

People who do not believe in God have tools for dealing with change; however, they have fewer tools than those who have God in their lives. To be without God must be similar to how the disciples felt during the storm on the Sea of Galilee, but without Jesus in the boat to wake up and rescue them.

Now consider all the tools that people of faith have at their disposal during similar times. There are certain spiritual values and principles that are more powerful than any temporal interests we might have. Spiritual methods of behavioral change, when they work, are like dynamite when compared with behavioral psychology methods alone.[80]

We choose to accept change if, and only if, we see how this new design enables us to contribute more to what we have defined as meaningful.[81] Spirituality and our search for meaning are intimately linked.

---

77. Livingston, 38.
78. Livingston, 33.
79. Rolheiser, 140.
80. William R. Miller, and John E. Martin eds. *Behavior Therapy and Religion: Integrating Spiritual And Behavioral Approaches to Change* (Newbury Park: Sage, 1988.), 27.
81. Ibid., 149.

Essential Components of a Sustaining Spirituality During Times of Change

Even though there is a growing movement of spirituality away from organized religion, the context of religion is a useful route to uncovering our sustaining spirituality during times of change.[82] Religion has been the most common route by which most people have been able to get in touch with their spirituality. It would seem that for Roman Catholics, the essential components of a sustaining spirituality during times of change would include Scripture, tradition and the sacraments, which we will examine in closer detail below.

The topic of the spirituality of change is so vast, and the material from which to draw so enormous, that all we can realistically hope to uncover in this examination is the merest sampling of relevant material. Let us now explore how the prophetic tradition of the Bible can inform our quest for spirituality during times of change.

Change in Scripture

Joseph Campbell, in *The Power of Myth,* identified a common myth that occurs in every culture.[83] He calls it the hero's journey. The myth is about personal enlightenment and collective renewal. The hero's journey is a story of individual transformation, a change of identity. In embarking on the journey, we must leave the world of certainty. To do this successfully, we must surrender our present self—we must step outside our old paradigms.[84]

Our Scriptures, both Hebrew and Christian, contain many accounts of hero journeys. These are the fountains from which we draw a great deal of our spirituality, the ways in which we live the human condition. Consequently, we will now turn our attention to the Scriptures, noting how they can inform our search for a spirituality that will sustain us during times of change within the Church. Once again, it must be noted that Scripture contains such a large body of material about how people adapted to changes that we can only realistically sample a fraction of the pertinent material.

---

82. David J. Tacey, *Remaking Men: Jung, Spirituality and Social Change* (New York: Routledge, 1997), 111.

83. Joseph Campbell, *The Power of Myth* (New York: Anchor Publishing, 1991), 39.

84. Quinn, 44-5.

Hebrew Scripture

Jeremiah as the Model Prophet for Spirituality During Times of Change

In the Hebrew Scriptures there are numerous stories of how people of faith dealt, for better or for worse, with changes. Many of the prophets referred to the exodus experience as they called people back to the torah/covenant. For those who might be going through major changes in their Church, the exodus experience might be an apt metaphor upon which to draw. This is but one example of how the prophetic history of the Hebrew Scriptures can provide fertile soil for discerning spirituality that will sustain us during times of change.

> Thus says the Lord: Stand by the roads, and look, and ask for the ancient paths, where the good way is; and walk in it, and find rest for your souls (Jer. 6:16).

Werner Lemke, in "The Prophets in a Time of Crisis," writes that those "ancient paths," of which the prophet here speaks, are the paths leading to the torah/covenant.[85] Jeremiah was the prophet during the second greatest event in the history of the Jewish people, the Babylonian Exile. He wrote during a time of great change and turmoil. There appears to be much that a sustaining spirituality during times of change can learn from Jeremiah and his messages to the people of his time.

One of the messages of the prophet Jeremiah, according to Robert Carroll in *From Chaos to Covenant*, is that "We must always relate to the past and be open to the future in constantly changing ways."[86] The relevance for the spirituality of change is obvious. Furthermore, Donald Gowan in *Theology of the Prophetic Books*, writes that "Exile and restoration became theological topics for the prophets."[87] Exile and restoration are apt models for the change experience, for in many ways people feel exiled when their Church is changing without them. On a much smaller scale, of course, the journey of a congregation leaving their Church and joining with another involves similar human dynamics. The personal impact of the closing of churches is a reality that any sustaining spirituality will need to address in forthcoming times of change.

Finally, Jeremiah's fourfold message of repentance, judgment, obedience and restoration, as Steven Fettke outlines it in *Messages to a Nation in Crisis*, provides

---

85. Werner E. Lemke, "The Prophets in a Time of Crisis," *Covenant Quarterly* 27 (Aug, 1969): 6.
86. Carroll, 277.
87. Donald E. Gowan, *Theology of the Prophetic Books: the Death and Resurrection of Israel* (Louisville: Westminster Press, 1998), 10.

a spiritually rich foundation upon which to discern some of the components of spiritual principles which will sustain us during times of change.[88]

Historical Context

Jeremiah was born into a priestly family in the country of Judah, under Assyrian influence. The people had turned away from the God of Israel and were practicing idolatry, which even included child sacrifice. Jeremiah's prophecies span 40 years in all. During this time, there was a reform of Judah and they turned away from their idolatry and back to God. This was short lived, however, and soon the people were back to worshiping idols. Eventually, Judah came under attack by the powerful Babylonian empire. Jeremiah saw this as God's judgment upon Judah for breaking the covenant. Judah ultimately fell to the Babylonians and many of its inhabitants were deported to Babylon. Judah became a vassal state of the vast Babylonian empire. Although he never lived to see it, Jeremiah told of the restoration of Judah which would come about seventy years later.

Admonitions

There are some serious cautions which emerge when citing the book of the Prophet Jeremiah. First, using Jeremiah's work as definitive for this age creates precisely one of the situations he was railing against: relying too heavily upon the dogma of the past as if it were the only definitive word.[89] Carroll might also agree that using Jeremiah's work in support of an institutional Church that practices oppression of any sort would be an insult to the prophet.[90] Whether that is the case here will be left up to the reader to decide.

There are also serious admonitions in the book of Jeremiah for anyone aspiring to be a prophet during times of change. Jeremiah condemns the false prophet Hananiah saying, "You have healed the people's wound too lightly by speaking a lie and making them believe what can do them no good" (Jer. 28:15). So, it would seem that to deliver a message about a sustaining spirituality that is intended only to make the people feel good during times of change would likewise bring down the prophet's condemnation.

Moreover, the Lord has spoken through the prophet, saying:

> "Behold, I am against those who prophesy lying dreams," says the LORD, "and who tell them and lead my people astray by their lies and their recklessness, when I did not send them or charge them; so they do not profit this people at all," says the LORD (Jer. 23:32).

---

88. Steven M. Fettke, *Messages to a Nation in Crisis: an Introduction to the Prophecy of Jeremiah* (Washington, D.C.: University Press of America, 1983), 21-49.

89. Carroll, 278.

90. Ibid.

Jeremiah's Fourfold Message

Using the four main messages of Jeremiah (judgment, repentance, obedience and restoration) as our guide, we will attempt to discern some of the principles which could inform a spirituality able to sustain us during times of change.[91]

Judgment

Jeremiah told the people of Judah that the Babylonian conquest and exile were the result of God's judgment upon the people for, among other things, worshiping the idols of the Assyrians.

> And I will utter my judgments against them, for all their wickedness in forsaking me; they have burned incense to other gods, and worshiped the works of their own hands (Jer. 1:14-16).

If we find that we are undergoing God's judgment, we can take heart in the fact that God withheld judgment from Judah for hundreds of years, hoping that the people might repent. Furthermore, in the midst of the judgment, like a loving father, God explained why the people were being punished (Jer. 4:18-6:13).

Most of the prophets named the oppression of their day as the reason for God's judgment. From Jeremiah's temple sermon in Chapter Seven we can deduce the oppressions of his day.

> For if you truly amend your ways and your doings, if you truly execute justice one with another, if you do not oppress the alien, the fatherless or the widow, or shed innocent blood in this place, and if you do not go after other gods to your own hurt (Jer. 7:5-6).

Judgment is a term avoided today in many religious circles because of its negative connotation. The concept of God's judgment is not viewed as being aligned with the kinder, gentler religion to which some religious people today subscribe. It may be helpful for such people to consider judgment in its broader form—not as punishment but as a way of God sifting, distinguishing and separating. It may simply be asking the question, How did this situation come about? In some cases, it is not God's judgment that brings about punishment, but internal circumstances that have their own naturally occurring negative consequences (e.g., when a person is caught driving drunk.)

As the prophet Jeremiah said, "Your ways and your doings have brought this upon you. This is your doom, and it is bitter; it has reached your very heart" (Jer. 4:18). It might be helpful, therefore, to reflect upon any systemic causes of the present circumstances.

---

91. Fettke, 29.

There has been a precipitous decline in the number of priests in the Roman Catholic Church over the past thirty years. This is due, in part at least, to the spirit of materialism and consumerism that has gripped the U. S. In 1980, the Sacred Congregation for the Clergy, part of the Roman Curia, also observed:

> We know that such disproportion [the ratio of priests to the general population] will probably get worse in the near future, and that the indifference of a large number of Catholics is increasing, also as a consequence of other evils, as secularism, naturalism, materialism, etc., which have pervaded the standard of living in countries of ancient Christian tradition.[92]

Nevertheless, it would seem that the Church cannot escape from its own responsibility for the present circumstances. The insistence on a male only, celibate priesthood has certainly exacerbated the precipitous decline in the ranks of the clergy. Bringing the focus more locally, those parishes struggling as a result of the priest shortage need to ask themselves, "What has this parish done to support vocations?"

Parishioners need to consider also what other role(s) they may have had in bringing about the current circumstances. It is clear that there has been a major shift in the way the majority of Catholic families view the possibility of their children entering religious life. Only fifty years ago, the occasion of a son entering the priesthood was a source of great joy and pride. Today, the mere mention of a vocation to the priesthood would most likely be met with the question, "Why would you want to do that?" In fact, as the priesthood is scandalized and continues to decline, one would expect parents to find more valid reasons to discourage vocations. It would appear that there is sufficient blame to go around and that the various circumstances mentioned here could have brought God's judgment down upon this age, if in fact the shortage of priests is God's judgment made manifest.

Scripture and tradition both teach us that change, even though painful, can be beneficial. The Babylonian Exile can be seen as an example. God told Jeremiah that the exile, which was God's judgment on the people, was necessary to rid Israel of its oppression of the poor. The exile brought about much pain and turmoil for the Jewish people. Quite ironically, the true Jewish identity belonged to the children of those who went into exile.[93] Those who remained in Israel during the exile were not considered the true Israelites any longer once those in exile

---

92. *Norms For Cooperation Among Local Churches And For a Better Distribution of The Clergy*, Sacred Congregation for the Clergy, *Postquam Apostoli*, 25 March, 1980, n. 11.

93. Gowan, 196.

returned. Those who were banished to Babylon experienced the pain necessary to bring about a change of heart in them, to amend their previously sinful ways and to return to the torah/covenant. This experience clearly impacted the formation of their children.

Repentance

To repent, as Jeremiah used the term, means to turn back, to turn away from the behavior that brought about God's judgment and to turn back to God and the torah/covenant. In Judah, during Jeremiah's time, they were practicing idol worship. To turn back, then, meant first to reject the idolatry they were practicing and then to return to worshiping the one true God. At the time, they were also oppressing the stranger, the orphans and the widow, and even practicing child sacrifice (Jer. 7:31). Is it any wonder that God brought down righteous judgment upon them?

From what are we called to repent? What is that from which we must turn away? First, we must repent of any of those areas we have previously identified as possible reasons for God's judgment. Conceivably, we may need to amend our materialistic ways. Maybe we should encourage, rather than discourage, our children from pursuing a vocation.

During Jeremiah's time, the people and the priests felt satisfied with the external practice of the law, but Jeremiah told them that the internal conversion of their hearts was more important. Jeremiah criticized people for placing their security on the temple's presence in their midst. Even the sacrifice in the temple could not (considering that the temple itself had become corrupt) assure the people protection if other elements in their lives were out of line with God's plan. Likewise, the early Christian missionary movement called upon the people to change the locus of their worship from the temple to the house churches.

Do we likewise need to reexamine our relationship with our Church buildings? Have we been worshiping another god, that is, our tenacious desire to hold on to our local Church buildings? Why do people give up going to Church entirely because their 11:30 A.M. Mass time was changed to 11:00 A.M.? Have we become more attached to our buildings, or a particular hour of the week, than to our faith in God? Are we worshiping the building—or a need for consistency—rather than our God? These are serious questions that people need to ask themselves if they find themselves tempted to forsake the worship of God in the midst of the changes we have ahead of us. As Lemke pointed out, Jeremiah commanded that, "The people were to trust in and obey Yahweh, not the building built to honor him."[94] Likewise, Derek Kidner in *The Message of Jeremiah* observes that "People have always focused more on holy objects than on holy

---

94. Lemke, 36.

living."[95] The temple in Jeremiah's time had actually become dishonored due to the way the people were using it. Is our resistance to change in the Church grounded in the fact that, as Lemke points out, we are, "Confusing worship of the one true God with the worship of our way of life?"[96]

Finally, in terms of repentance, we need to ask ourselves the question, "Have we become only external worshipers?" We need always to beware of false religiosity, that is, isolating religion from the rest of our lives.

The Way of Obedience

We must replace those behaviors and attitudes from which we are repenting with obedience. Jeremiah told the people that they must conform themselves to God's torah/covenant. Jeremiah even told the people that to obey meant to surrender to the Babylonians. This brought about much hardship.

To obey meant to practice justice, which for Jeremiah's community meant not to murder; to take care of the aliens, widows and orphans; and to stop worshiping idols.

This is what the Lord requires of us, according to Isaiah 1:17: "Cease to do evil, learn to do good, seek justice, correct oppressions, defend the fatherless, plead for the widow." We need to focus on living lives of justice and fidelity, not becoming preoccupied with the relatively minor inconveniences to which we may be called to adjust. Ultimately, we need to stop focusing on what is being done to us (such as the Church taking away our priest or a convenient location or a favored Mass time) and start focusing on what we are doing in furtherance of that which God requires of us. Perhaps this is why it is so threatening to have our churches closed: because the only worship we know is in a building at a particular hour of the week, rather than in our hearts and in our interactions with our brothers and sisters. Of what ultimate benefit could it be for us if we fight tooth and nail for our perceived needs, for our Church building, when the net result might be that our brothers or sisters have to suffer and we have no regard for their suffering? We might dishonor the Sabbath in God's eyes every time we walked into that church.

The book of the prophet Jeremiah is the story of God's unrequited love. God uses the image of a married couple to describe the relationship between Israel and God, and refers to Israel as a harlot. Nevertheless, God would take Israel back in an instant if only she would turn away from the evil she is doing.

Restoration

As was discussed previously, one of the multitude of reasons people resist change is that on some level their identity is being threatened. In order to assist members of

---

95. Derek Kidner, *The Message of Jeremiah: Against Wind and Tide* (Downers Grove: Inter-Varsity Press, 1987), 98.

96. Lemke, 16.

congregations to find an identity which is not threatened or undermined in times of change, Robert Kysar proposes that congregations consider adopting this as their identity statement: "We are a community of faith, on the way home, stumbling in the light."[97] The home to which we are journeying is the future filled with hope.

In their darkest hours, as the Babylonian horde was breaking through the city gates, God through Jeremiah promised the people a future filled with hope. "For I know the plans I have for you, says the LORD, plans for welfare and not for evil, to give you a future and a hope" (Jer. 29:11).

As the Babylonians were storming the gates of Jerusalem, Jeremiah purchased land that the Babylonians had already captured (Jer. 32:6-16). He bought this land as a prophetic sign of hope in the future that things would eventually return to the way God intended them. This hope was totally grounded in God. It was not a naive belief that everything would work out. It was a sure hope that God was fulfilling promises even in the midst of God's judgment. Jeremiah's hope was resolute even with the certainty of their defeat sealed.

Jeremiah prophesied for 40 years. During that time, he was hated by the people, denounced as a traitor, rejected by his family, tortured and imprisoned. He saw his people conquered and taken off to Babylon, and yet he had sufficient hope to purchase land which he died without ever seeing.

We must practice the sort of hope Jeremiah demonstrated. In the midst of the pain, despair and gloom that might come upon us as major change in the Church is going on, we need to take an action we would normally take as if we were members of our ideal Church. We need to act as if everything for which we could ever hope is already here in the Church. If we claim it and work for it, together with God, it can someday become true.

The message of the prophets, according to Robert Carroll, is that, "There is not, and cannot be, any permanent security, whether in theology, ideology, nationalism, patriotism, ritual, ancestry, history or whatever."[98] Likewise, there is not and cannot be any permanent security in our priests or our Church buildings. Permanent security can only come from that which is eternal, the Lord our God.

Christian Gospel

How Jesus Personally Adapted to Change

As William Herzog noted in *Jesus, Justice and the Reign of God*, the Christian Gospels model that which has been "The challenge of the ages, to search for the historical Jesus in light of the struggles of this day and how his life might speak to

---

97.   Kysar, 35.
98.   Carroll, 277.

those struggles."[99] We now turn our attention specifically to Jesus and to the spiritual means by which he adapted to change as revealed by Scripture. This is a task well worth undertaking since, as George Jeffrey wrote "In Change, Unchanged": "The power of Jesus to call forth the best from the human heart has been proved over the centuries."[100]

While Scripture does not explicitly indicate that Jesus used spiritual tools to adapt to the changes going on around him, it certainly does portray him employing many spiritual tools. Circumstances would dictate, though, that in many cases Jesus used these spiritual tools in response to some change that had happened or was about to happen in his life.

Scripture notes several times when Jesus went off by himself to pray. The first such occurrence was right after John baptized him. He went off into the wilderness for forty days (Mt. 4:1-11). The deprivation of the desert helped him to realize that God was the only true source of his identity.[101]

Likewise, after he heard of John's death, Jesus withdrew to be alone (Mt. 14:13). After He healed a leper, Jesus' fame spread. Large crowds gathered around him to hear him preach and to be healed, but he went off again to be alone and pray (Lk. 5:16). Similarly, when he learned that the people were going to seize him to make him their king, Jesus went off to the mountain by himself (Jn. 6:15). When faced with what was arguably the biggest change in his life, his impending death, again Jesus went off to be alone. Even though he took three of the apostles with him, he left them and went off a little farther to be alone and pray (Mt. 26:39). There are other examples of this (Lk. 6:12-13 & Mk. 1:35), which demonstrate the value Jesus placed on solitude and prayer.

Another means by which he dealt with change was by practicing compassion. Jesus had compassion for those who pursued him (Mt 14:14) and set aside his desire to be alone in order to minister to their needs.

In the garden of Gethsemane, Jesus also practiced obedience to God in the face of great and certainly painful change. "If it be possible, let this cup pass from me; nevertheless, not as I will, but as thou wilt" (Mt. 26:39).

Not only did obedience sustain him during times of change, but clearly his faith and trust in God supported him, too. His commitment was demonstrated to the very end of his life when he stretched out his arms on the cross.

Finally, Jesus had those with whom he was intimate, the apostles. Although at times they challenged and taxed his energy and patience, one could imagine them

99. William R. Herzog, II. *Jesus, Justice and the Reign of God* (Louisville: Westminster, 2000), 252.

100. George J. Jeffrey, "In Change, Unchanged," *Expository Times* 62 (1950): 56.

101. Ford, 43.

supporting Jesus and one another during the life changes they all experienced. That was perhaps the reason why Jesus took Peter, James and John with him to the garden of Gethsemane.

Just as we are justified by faith and not by works, so, too, people do not change themselves, but are changed by looking at a situation differently—sometimes by believing in God's solution, Jesus Christ.[102] Using the foregoing examples of Christ spiritually adapting to change, we will now attempt to construct a modern day practical application for the spiritual ways in which Jesus adapted to change.

Jesus often sought solitude and prayed. Those struggling to deal with change would do well to heed Jesus' words to "Pray always, and not lose heart," (Lk. 18:1). The power of prayer can be neither underestimated nor overstated here. It is the lifeblood of those seeking to live the spiritual life. It is that which will sustain us during those times of trial that change often engenders.

That Jesus sought solitude should be similarly instructive to us. A spiritual retreat during a tumultuous time of change can be just the antidote for the fear that often attends changes. Spiritual retreats can provide the "time out" from our cluttered, jam-packed, modern lives, to develop a true perspective about that which has passed away and that which has replaced it. Retreats can provide the necessary space to grieve the losses that always accompany changes, so that we can go back into the world with the necessary enthusiasm for that which God is continuously creating and bringing about. Finally, the deprivation that the retreat attempts to create can lead to both creativity and recognition that God is the only true source of our identity.[103] An appreciation and acceptance of this reality may be the precious jewel contained within the struggle a parish or diocese may face when closing a Church building. Our spiritual identity is in God, not in any particular building and not with any particular minister.

Just as Jesus was compassionate toward others even when he wanted to be alone, we, too, must be compassionate toward our leaders and those who seek to bring about change. We must fight against our initial urge to attack those who wish to initiate or respond to changes, so that we can gain the necessary perspective (and this takes time, sometimes a lot of time) to discern the true value of the change. In every case, though, following Christ's example, we need to put a higher premium on our relationships with others than upon the inconvenience change may bring into our lives.

When Jesus was faced with his impending death, His desire was not to suffer. Nevertheless, he obediently submitted himself to God's will. Sometimes, when all

---

102. Paul Deschenes and Martha L. Rogers. "A Systems View of Jesus as Change Agent." *Journal of Psychology & Theology* 9 (Sum., 1981): 129.

103. Ford, 43.

other spiritual means have been exhausted and we still find ourselves resisting inevitable change, we may have to say likewise: "Not as I will, but as thou wilt" (Mt. 26:39).

Suffering may be the result of changes going on in the Church. If we must suffer, let us look upon such suffering as Paul wrote about it:

> More than that, we rejoice in our sufferings, knowing that suffering produces endurance, and endurance produces character, and character produces hope, and hope does not disappoint us, because God's love has been poured into our hearts through the Holy Spirit which has been given to us (Rom. 5:3-5).

The proper attitude toward suffering joins us to the suffering Christ endured, thereby making our suffering redemptive.

Just as Jesus was committed to the end, engaging in change requires a higher level of commitment from all members of the Church.[104] We really need to examine the extent to which we are committed to the future of the Church, through the "good" and "bad" change. If we find that our commitment is somewhat lacking, we would do well to reexamine Christ's commitment to us and to the Church. In this we might find the measure of spiritual strength needed to sustain us in times of change.

Jesus had those with whom he was intimate and these relationships gave him strength. We need intimates in our lives as well, for a host of reasons. Among these reasons is that we can go to these intimates to process the feelings that attend any major change. The way to get past feelings such as anger, sadness and anxiety (which are all normal when we are faced with change) is not to try to avoid them, but to go through them. Working these feelings out with intimates is one way we can get to the point where we can begin to think rationally about the changes and our possible responses. If we attend to this work, we might find the excitement, anticipation (in a good sense), and the joy that can also accompany changes.

There is certainly plenty of reason in today's society to adopt a gloom and doom mentality; however, as the people called to be filled with hope in the future, we do God, our Church, ourselves and those around us a great disservice by focusing only on the bad at the expense of seeing the good. The Sacred Congregation for the Clergy said this best:

> The situation of the Church today, especially as regards the insufficiency of clergy for the most urgent needs of evangelization, could induce many to a pessimistic vision of things and thus create a certain sense of

---

104. Nancy Tatom Ammerman, "Congregations In The Midst Of Change: An Interview," *Christian Century* 114 (Jan. 15, 97): 50.

discouragement toward the future of the Church. Such a way of thinking is not the way of Christians and even less becoming to pastors of souls.[105]

The antidote for gloom and doom is found in Paul's second letter to the Corinthians:

> So we do not lose heart. Though our outer nature is wasting away, our inner nature is being renewed every day. For this slight momentary affliction is preparing for us an eternal weight of glory beyond all comparison, because we look not to the things that are seen but to the things that are unseen; for the things that are seen are transient, but the things that are unseen are eternal (2 Cor 4:16-18).

In spite of huge changes in the Church over the past two thousand years, Christ's message is still touching hearts and healing wounds. Christian freedom allows us to live in the holy moment, for the future is in God's hands. As Jesus said, "Therefore do not be anxious about tomorrow, for tomorrow will be anxious for itself. Let the day's own trouble be sufficient for the day" (Mt. 6:34).

We need to find sustenance in Jesus' promise to be "With us, even to the end of time" (Mt. 28:20). We need to act as if Jesus is standing right next to us every moment of our lives, for, in fact, He is.

Change and Conflict in the Christian Scriptures

Any significant change in the Church is going to create conflict. Consequently, our search for a spirituality to sustain us during times of change in the Church must consider productive approaches to the inevitable conflict that will accompany such change.

In *Building Community*, Sofield, et al., write that conflict is a Christian reality.[106] This flies in the face of the common idealized perception Christians have about their own communities. Certainly only those Christians most in denial will dispute the idea that conflicts exist in their communities. With songs like *They Will Know We Are Christians by Our Love* ringing in their ears, many would deny the necessity for conflict transformation programs or processes.

Jesus and Conflict

The story of Jesus is the story of the many conflicts he encountered.[107] The types of conflict with which Jesus dealt can be broken down into four general

---

105. Congregation for the Clergy, n. 31.

106. Loughlan Sofield, Rosine Hammett and Carroll Juliano, *Building Community: Christian, Caring, Vital* (Notre Dame: Ave Maria Press, 1998), 78.

107. Ford, 253.

categories: "fundamental, unavoidable, essential, and incidental."[108] Jesus' response to each of these conflicts was measured according to his mission. It was Jesus' relative lack of inner conflict that freed him to deal creatively with the external conflicts he encountered.[109]

Fundamental conflicts were defining moments for Jesus, such as his encounter with the devil during his forty days in the wilderness (Mt. 4:1-11), and all those instances when he cast out evil spirits (Mk. 1:21-26; 9:14-29, Lk. 11:18-22). His nature and the nature of his mission were fundamentally incompatible with the devil's nature. Jesus' response to these encounters was to stand and fight. The weapons he employed were: unwavering resistance, prayers, and citing Scripture.[110]

Unavoidable conflicts generally occurred with Jesus over issues of power and control, in almost all cases with the religious leaders of his day. These happened in Capernaum, when Jesus forgave the paralytic man's sins and then healed him, all in the presence of the Scribes (Mk. 2:7). A little while later, the Scribes criticized him again for eating with tax collectors (Mk. 2:16). On another occasion, the Pharisees criticized him for allowing his disciples to eat grain from the field on the Sabbath (Mk. 2:23-28).

Perhaps Jesus' most dramatic response to conflict, actually a conflict that he initiated, was the incident known as the cleansing of the temple (Mt. 21:12-13). Jesus, by this prophetic action, was proclaiming the need for change.[111] His actions and words were an attack on the economic, political and religious system of his day.[112] Specifically, he was condemning the priestly aristocracy that had put heavy burdens on an already overburdened people.

Jesus' response to unavoidable conflicts was to face them squarely and seize the opportunity they represented. When the Pharisees criticized him for healing the man with the withered hand on the Sabbath (Mk. 3:4), Jesus did not get caught up in the minutiae, but focused on the bigger picture, freeing people from oppression. When the Pharisees again attempted to trip him up by asking, "Is it all right to pay Caesar's tax?" (Mt. 22:15), Jesus seized the opportunity to communicate his vision again. The attitude he brought to these conflicts was that even if the one with whom he was in conflict was not won over, others sitting by quietly and listening might be persuaded to change.[113]

---

108. Ford, 258.
109. Ibid., 254.
110. Ibid., 258.
111. Paula Fontana Qualls, "Mark 11:15-18 : A Prophetic Challenge." *Review & Expositor* 93 (Sum, 1999): 395.
112. Ibid., 401.
113. Ford, 266.

Jesus viewed essential conflicts as necessary in order for people to learn. In many cases these occurred with his followers. When they squabbled over who was the greatest (Mk. 9:34), when they disagreed about who could belong (Mk. 9:38), and when they were unable to heal a boy, (Mk. 9:18), Jesus' response was to sit and teach them. When they argued over who was the greatest, Jesus used this as an opportunity to teach: "If any one would be first, he must be last of all and servant of all" (Mk. 9:35). Later, when the disciples became indignant over James and John asking to sit at the right and left hand of Jesus, he used this opportunity to teach them all about the proper exercise of power (Mk. 10:42-45).

Incidental conflicts were those not connected with his primary mission: for instance, the conflict with his family when they thought that he had gone crazy (Mk. 3:21). In another incidental conflict, the people of his own hometown became so enraged over something he said that they tried to throw him off a cliff (Lk. 4:29). Jesus' response to incidental conflict was to walk away and wait. Jesus avoided the Samaritan village that would not welcome him, because this was not a fight that would have furthered his mission (Lk. 9:51-55). Borrowing the words of a familiar song, when it came to responding to conflicts Jesus knew "When to hold 'em, [knew] when to fold 'em, [knew] when to walk away and [knew] when to run."[114]

The Gentile Conflict in the Early Christian Community

We will now turn our attention to the struggle of the early Christian community over the conditions for admission of the Gentiles. As we shall see, this was a deeply divisive and pivotal issue for the community. Had the ultimate decision been different, it is certain that Christianity, as we know it today, would not exist. It is even conceivable that the good news of Jesus Christ as practiced by the early Church might have eventually died out, like so many other upstart Jewish sects of its day.

Before we get into the background of the conflict, we have to acknowledge the problem of the sources for information on this dispute over admission requirements for Gentiles. Information about this conflict was obtained from Scripture as well as modern scriptural commentaries. Our scriptural material comes from the Acts of the Apostles and Paul's letter to the community at Galatia. The main problem with these scriptural sources is that they were not necessarily written with the intention of relaying historical facts, but were written for certain communities with particular issues at certain places in time. Surprisingly, there are many similarities between the two accounts of the council in Jerusalem where this issue was eventually decided. Nevertheless, there are many points of divergence as well. The Acts of the Apostles account of the final decision at the Jerusalem Council was that Gentiles should not have to be circumcised, but that they

---

114. Kenny Rogers, *The Gambler*.

should follow a few of the dietary and sexual continency laws. Paul's letter makes no mention of this compromise. Consequently, we are left with having to decide which, if either, of the sources is closer to the truth. The one undeniable fact, based upon modern evidence, is that Gentiles were allowed at some point in time into the early Christian community.

The problem with modern scriptural commentaries is that they are a combination of uncertain scriptural sources and educated guesses on the part of their authors. Even more discrepancies are found in the commentaries. Raymond Brown and John Meier, for instance, write in *Antioch and Rome: New Testament Cradles of Catholic Christianity* that Paul's letter to the Galatians should be our primary source for material about the Jerusalem Council, since Luke was trying to present a harmonious picture.[115] Other commentators maintain just the opposite, that the Acts account should be considered the more reliable source.

Having now established the uncertainty of our sources, we have to acknowledge that these are the sources we have. Even non-scriptural first century material presents the same problem as scriptural material: they were not necessarily written with the intention of relaying historical facts, but were written for certain communities with particular issues at certain points in time. We will have to accept these accounts at face value and attempt to reconcile any glaring discrepancies that may impact the conflict or the resolution process.

In order to understand the nature of the conflict over admission of the Gentiles into the early Christian community, we must first understand the first century Jewish belief concerning Gentiles. Generally speaking, the Jewish people regarded themselves as a race of people chosen by God to the exclusion of all others. "The Lord is merciful and gracious" (Ps. 2:5); for the Jewish people this meant that the Lord is only gracious to the Israelites. As for the other nations, God will terrify. Jewish people could not eat anything that died of natural causes, but could sell it to the Gentile. The reason given was simply, "For you are a people holy to the LORD your God" (Dt. 14:21). During the sabbatical year (every seventh year), the Jewish people were to forgive other Jewish people any debts owed them; they did not have to forgive the debts owed to them by Gentiles (Dt. 15:3).

On the other hand, there are parts of the Hebrew Scriptures where the Jewish people were commanded to treat the Gentile with acceptance and compassion. "When a stranger sojourns with you in your land, you shall not do him wrong. The stranger who sojourns with you shall be to you as the native among you, and you shall love him as yourself; for you were strangers in the land of Egypt" (Lv. 19:33-34). By the time of the first century, however, the Jewish people had embraced

---

115. Raymond E. Brown and John P. Meier, *Antioch and Rome: New Testament Cradles of Catholic Christianity* (New York: Paulist Press, 1983), 36.

statutes that excluded the Gentiles and set them outside of God's love, and had disregarded those statutes that commanded them to love the stranger among them.

There are numerous direct and indirect references to the Gentiles in the gospel accounts of Jesus' life. Matthew's gospel, written primarily for a Jewish audience, contains many pejorative references to the Gentiles. "And in praying do not heap up empty phrases as the Gentiles do; for they think that they will be heard for their many words. Do not be like them, for your Father knows what you need before you ask him" (Mt. 6:8-9). In the exchange between Jesus and the Canaanite woman, he refers to the Gentiles as dogs. "But she came and knelt before him, saying 'Lord, help me.' And he answered, 'It is not fair to take the children's bread and throw it to the dogs'" (Mt. 15:24-26). Finally, Jesus uses the common practice of shunning the Gentile to explain what to do with someone among them who refuses to repent of a wrong done. "If he refuses to listen to them, tell it to the Church; and if he refuses to listen even to the Church, let him be to you as a Gentile and a tax collector" (Mt. 18:17-18).

Once again, as in the examples from the Hebrew Scriptures, there are positive references to be found in Matthew's gospel. Jesus said, "I tell you, many will come from east and west and sit at table with Abraham, Isaac and Jacob in the kingdom of heaven, while the sons of the kingdom will be thrown into the outer darkness; there men will weep and gnash their teeth" (Mt. 8:11-13). The phrase "who come[s] from east and west" refers to the Gentiles while "the sons of the kingdom" refers to the chosen people, the Israelites. Matthew's gospel also indicates that Jesus "shall proclaim justice to the Gentiles…and in his name will the Gentiles hope" (Mt. 12:20-21).

The presence of Gentiles in the early Christian community created a problem. There were those in the early Christian community who, like many of the Jewish people of their day, ignored the many positive examples of Christ toward the Gentiles and chose to embrace only the pejorative references. Their religious formation predisposed them to believe that only the Jewish people, the "Chosen people," could be saved. Consequently, they felt that before a Gentile could enter into the early Christian community, that person first had to become an observant Jew (Acts. 15:1, 5). Since this was not happening, it created a major dilemma for strict Jewish members of the early Church. Since observant Jews could not have anything to do with Gentiles, could not have Gentiles as guests or even eat a meal with them, this created many uncomfortable encounters in the early Church. This was a problem that needed to be solved, but it did not lend itself to an easy solution.

According to the Acts of the Apostles, Peter was the first to wrestle with this issue when he was summoned to the home of Cornelius, a Roman Centurion (Acts. 10:22). When Cornelius invited him in, Peter crossed the threshold between adhering to the strict Jewish customs of his day in favor of embracing the call of the Gospel. Peter's pronouncement to Cornelius makes his position clear: "Truly I perceive that God shows no partiality, but in every nation anyone who fears him and does what is right is acceptable to him" (Acts. 10:35).

When Peter returned to Jerusalem from this encounter with Cornelius, he was roundly criticized for breaking with Jewish custom (Acts. 11:2-3). Peter's response to this was to tell the entire story over again. While it might make sense that Peter in fact told this story more than once, it is astonishing that the author of Acts chose to write the story a second time. Since space was at a premium on the parchment rolls upon which Scripture was written in the first century, this underscores the importance attached to this issue in the early Christian community. They could very well have seen this as a "make it or break it" issue for the emerging Church.

In Antioch of Pisidia, according to the Acts of the Apostles, Paul and Barnabas came into conflict with the Jews as a result of their preaching to the Gentiles, as well as their condemnation of the Jewish people (Acts. 13:45-50). Eventually, Paul and Barnabas were driven from that region over this issue. From this point on until the Council of Jerusalem, Paul and Barnabas are constantly harassed by the Jews; in fact, at one point Paul was stoned until the people thought he was dead (Acts 14:19). It is unclear here whether the Jews with whom they came into conflict were observant Jewish members of the early Christian community or Jewish people outside of the faith. Nevertheless, this highlights once again the extreme emotion evoked in the Jewish people of that time over dealings with the Gentiles.

This entire issue became preeminent when some of the strict Jews from the early Christian community traveled to Antioch and attempted to convince Paul's converts that they would lose everything unless they first became observant Jews. Paul and Barnabas argued strongly against this but to no avail. This was an issue that was going to have to be decided by the elders of the early Christian community. Paul and Barnabas traveled to Jerusalem to consult with the apostles. This has been euphemistically referred to as the "Jerusalem Council."

According to Brown and Meier, four distinct groups were parties to this dispute.[116] First, there were those members of the early Christian community who believed that a follower of Christ must fully observe all Jewish laws including circumcision. They are referred to in Acts as the "Sect of the Pharisees," and "Circumcision Party," and by Paul, in his letters, as "false brothers," and "spies."

The second distinct group was comprised of those who did not feel that it was necessary to circumcise male Gentile converts to Christianity, but believed that they should follow some of the Jewish laws. This was the compromise solution proffered by James which was eventually to become the decision of the "Jerusalem Council."

---

116. Brown & Meier, 1-9.

The third group, according to Brown and Meier, was those who did not feel that the Gentiles had to conform with any of the Jewish laws. Paul was probably a member of this group or the next. The last party to this dispute believed that the Gentiles were not subject to Jewish laws and did not see any purpose in celebrating Jewish feasts.

At the Jerusalem Council Paul and Barnabas simply tell the story of what had happened. They let the facts speak for themselves. On the other hand, some of the Pharisees who had presumably become Christians insisted that all converts must be circumcised and abide by the Jewish laws. The principle or value at stake was fundamental. Was the gift of God for the select few or for the whole world?

Supporting Paul and Barnabas, Peter then spoke and reminded the assembly that God had already revealed, through Peter himself, that the Gentiles should be part of the early Christian community. Presumably this was a reference to Peter's encounter with Cornelius, the Roman Centurion, and the subsequent confrontation by the "Circumcision Party" (discussed earlier.)

After Paul and Barnabas revealed to the gathering of apostles and elders all the "signs and wonders" that God had performed for the Gentiles, James offered his perspective. In it, he cited Amos 9:11-12 as proof from the Hebrew Scriptures that the Gentiles were to be eventually incorporated into the chosen people. This was probably added in an attempt to satisfy the circumcision party.[117]

Although Scripture has James proclaiming a judgment, it is more likely that this was just his opinion that was eventually accepted by the assembly of apostles and elders. James' opinion was that Gentiles should not be required to follow the majority of the Jewish law with the exception of some dietary and sexual practice laws. Bruce maintains that James had the final word because Peter's reputation had been compromised by his previous association with Gentiles.[118]

Paul and Barnabas, along with two reputable witnesses, were then sent back to Antioch with a letter outlining the decision rendered by the Jerusalem Council. Such was the depth of the disagreement that presumably Paul needed independent witnesses to prove the truth of this letter to the community in Antioch. Shortly after this, Acts describes a disagreement between Paul and Barnabas that caused them to go their separate ways.

Paul's version of the Jerusalem Council, remarkable in its many similarities to the account in Acts, has a slightly different rendering of the decision (Gal. 2:1-10). The letter to the Galatians simply gives Paul the continued blessing of the elders to preach the Gospel to the uncircumcised and Peter the mission to preach

---

117. F. F. Bruce, *Peter, Stephen, James, and John: Studies in Early Non-Pauline Christianity* (Grand Rapids: W. B. Eerdmans, 1979), 93-94.
118. Ibid., 92.

to the circumcised. The only requirement for Paul and the communities to which he preached was to remember the poor.

Paul goes on to describe a confrontation between him and Peter in Antioch over table fellowship with the Gentiles. The trouble was by no means over. Part of the life of the early Christian community was a common meal which they called the Agape or Love Feast. At this meal the entire congregation came together to enjoy a common meal by combining their resources. In a very special way, it symbolized the unity of the Christian community.

Since this comes after what is presumably Paul's account of the Jerusalem Council, we could surmise that the conflict was far from resolved in Jerusalem. It is also possible that the confrontation with Peter and the "men [that] came from James" could have been the precursor to the Jerusalem Council. In either case, Paul describes Peter eating with the Gentiles until these men from James arrived. At that point Peter and the rest of the Jewish Christians separated themselves from the Gentiles, "fearing the circumcision party" (Gal. 2:12). This would imply that James was in fact the leader of the circumcision party and that Peter was certainly not as resolute in his stand for the Gentiles as the account in Acts describes him.

This story does point out something about which the Jerusalem Council was silent. While it was agreed that the Gentiles should not be burdened by having to comply with Jewish law, were Jewish Christians allowed to interact with them, since this, too, was contrary to the Jewish laws? If the Jerusalem council did not resolve this issue, then clearly this dispute was far from resolved for the early Christian community as Paul's letter to the Galatians may have demonstrated. It is interesting to note that Galatians has Paul and Barnabas separating over the issue of shared table fellowship with the Gentiles, once again highlighting the unsettled nature of the conflict.

Conflict and change are the conjoined twins of life. It is the rare occasion when we would find a situation of change without any attendant conflict. The method by which we resolve or do not resolve conflicts reflects our spirituality. Consequently, on the face of it, good conflict transformation strategies should provide us with more spiritual tools to use in positively adapting to change.

Jesus encouraged his disciples with the words, "Fear not, little flock, for it is your Father's good pleasure to give you the kingdom" (Lk. 12:32). It is clear that as a people, Christians are still growing into their understanding and acceptance of these words of reassurance, and that whenever we have to face the inevitability of change and conflict in the Church, we would do well to remind ourselves of these words of Christ.

Change in Tradition

Believing that the Holy Spirit has been ever present in guiding the Church since Pentecost and throughout the ages, Roman Catholics draw heavily from the tradition/history of the Church. The prophets of the Hebrews constantly called upon Israel's past, pointing out the many good things God has done and then suggesting how people should respond. So, too, Roman Catholics rely upon our rich heritage to inform our spirituality. Given that the Church has gone through countless transformations over its almost two thousand year history, there is much here to be gained in the effort to identify spirituality during times of change.

<u>Church Councils</u>

All Church councils have involved change of some sort. Many have involved wholesale disputes over relevant doctrinal matters of their day, while some addressed pastoral practices of their day. The Fourth Lateran Council of 1215, for instance, decreed that Catholics must receive Holy Communion as a matter of obligation during the Easter Season. This was in response to the infrequent reception of the Eucharist due to a sense of reverence and unworthiness on the part of the recipients.

A complete treatment of the changes triggering and resulting from the Church councils would be a book unto itself and well beyond the scope of this inquiry. Suffice it to say, though, that change has been the ever present companion of the Church throughout the ages, and this has been particularly evident in our history of Church councils.

We can benefit from a brief examination of our most recent Church council, Vatican II. From 1962-1965 the Roman Catholic Church gathered for its twenty-first Church Council. The beloved Pope John XXIII, the pontiff who called the Church together for this council, said in his opening remarks: "[The Church] must ever look to the present, to the new conditions and new forms of life introduced into the modern world, which have opened new avenues to the Catholic apostolate."[119] Clearly, this can happen only as long as we remain open, trusting, and faithful in the midst of change.

He pointed out how change actually frees us for our most important task, meditating upon higher matters. "By bringing herself up to date where required, and by the wise organization of mutual co-operation, the Church will make men (sic), families, and peoples really turn their minds to heavenly things."[120] With

---

119. Pope John XXIII's address on the occasion of the opening of the Second Vatican Council, October 11, 1962.
120. Ibid.

that, the Council set out to impart an ever-increasing vigor to the Christian life of the faithful; to adapt more closely to the needs of their age those institutions they believed were subject to change.[121]

The various documents issued by the Council indicated that the bishops were indeed listening to the Holy Father and concurred with his view of the necessary changes required for the Church. In the *Dogmatic Constitution on the Church*, the Council Fathers wrote:

> Episcopal conferences should ensure that periodically there are refresher courses on the Bible and in spiritual and pastoral theology, so that amid all the change and flux the clergy will acquire a deeper knowledge of theology and of pastoral methods.[122]

Finally, in its *Decree on the Training of the Priests*, the Council again highlighted the symbiotic relationship between continuity and change:

> It (The Council) lays down certain fundamental principles, wherein regulations already tested by the experience of centuries are reaffirmed, and new regulations are introduced, in harmony with the constitutions and decrees of the sacred Council and the changed conditions of our times.[123]

While the current Pontiff is seen by many as highly conservative and responsible for a retrenchment away from many of the Vatican II reforms, he has recently pointed out the need for changes in the Church, at least on the parish level, when he wrote, "The parish is in need of constant renewal."[124]

Reformation Spirituality

The Reformation was clearly a time of great change in the Church. The reformers and their followers did not set out to create a new Church but to reform what they saw as the excesses and perversions of the Church of their time. Nevertheless, they found themselves on the outside looking in, separated from the only Church that they had known and loved. The spirituality which they developed and practiced at that time can offer much to our quest for a sustaining spirituality during times of change. This consideration of reformation spirituality

---

121. *Constitution on the Sacred Liturgy*, 1.
122. *Decree on the Church's Missionary Activity*, Vatican II, *Ad Gentes Divinitus* (7 December, 1965), #19.
123. *Decree on the Training of Priests*, Vatican II, *Optatam Totius*, (28 October, 1965).
124. John Paul II, *Post Synodal Apostolic Exhortation Christifideles Laici* (30 December 1988), 26.

can only scratch the surface of this vast topic, as was the case with our examination of Church councils.

Reformation spirituality was more than just a return to Scripture.[125] It was a recognition that God's redemptive act in Christ was and is relevant to everyday life.

The Reformation criticized inauthentic forms of spirituality.[126] They rejected the notion that somehow the priests were more spiritual than the people and upheld the priesthood of the laity by virtue of their Baptism. Parenthetically, most of the lay ministry performed in the Catholic Church today is consistent with this premise. Since the declining numbers of priests will necessitate more lay ministry, this aspect of reformation spirituality seems particularly relevant.

The reformers also rejected any notion of a theology detached from the lived experience of the people. The quest for a theology of change, a way for people to encounter God in the midst of the changes going on in their lives, is consistent with this reformation ideal.

The foundation of reformation spirituality was grounded and nourished by Scripture.[127] Incidentally, this is entirely consistent with Benedictine and Ignatian spirituality, as well. There was not a wholesale rejection of doctrine, just doctrine that was inconsistent with Scripture, such as indulgences, a major point of contention for the reformers.

The reformers wanted to make Scripture understandable by applying it to the lives of the people by way of the sermon. They brought together Scripture and theology. Our search for identity, authenticity, and fulfillment in the midst of change is not separate from, but intricately linked to, God. Who we are and what we are is connected with who and what God is.[128] This raises the importance of knowing Jesus Christ as revealed by Scripture. Spirituality firmly rooted in Scripture and theology is a check against purely personally developed spiritual practices.[129]

Many scholars, Catholic and Protestant alike, agree that the Protestant Reformation, although painful, was a necessary change for the Church of its time. The same can be said for the recent reforms of the Second Vatican Council. Vatican II, unconsciously or perhaps consciously, recognized the wisdom of many of the reformers' goals and ideals, albeit 400 years later. The Second Vatican Council likewise held up the centrality of Scripture in the spiritual life of the faithful, the importance of the active role of the laity in the Church, and the

---

125. McGrath, 18.

126. Ibid., 34.

127. Ibid., 42.

128. William R. Miller, *Living As If: How Positive Faith Can Change Your Life* (Philadelphia: Westminster, 1985), 48.

129. Ibid., 51.

equal holiness of the call to the priesthood and the call to live a sanctified life as a lay person.[130]

There is real irony, and no small measure of hope, in the fact that this Roman Catholic writer, who as a child had to ask permission to attend the wedding of a close relative in a Presbyterian Church and was strongly cautioned against any active participation in that service, can now feel free to promote Reformation spirituality to Roman Catholics struggling with change in the Church. It is likewise a testament to, and evidence of, the tremendous change already visited upon the Roman Catholic Church in the last forty or so years.

Change in Sacraments

Finally, the Catholic Church is a sacramental Church. Contained within the theology of the sacraments is material that can enlighten our search for a spirituality during times of change. As for the practical, people receive many of the sacraments at major transition points in their life, such as adult Baptism, Marriage, Confirmation, Holy Orders, and the Anointing of the Sick. In many ways, we sacramentalize our change. Even the regular (as opposed to one time) sacraments of Eucharist and Penance are available for spiritual nourishment and sustenance during times of struggle with change.

Baptism captures one of the central paradoxes of the Christian faith. When those baptized go into the water, they are said to have died to sin. When they come out of the water, they are said to have risen with Christ.

We read in Mark's Gospel that, "Jesus began to show his disciples that he must go to Jerusalem and suffer many things from the elders and chief priests and scribes, and be killed, and on the third day be raised" (Mt. 16:21). Of course, this was not something the disciples wanted to hear. Paul wrote along the same lines, "For while we live we are always being given up to death for Jesus' sake, so that the life of Jesus may be manifested in our mortal flesh. So death is at work in us, but life in you" (2 Cor. 4:11-12).

Even as people of faith, nowhere do we feel more abandoned than at the moment of our death or the death of a loved one. Yet, as Christians, we believe in a life hereafter where the worst days in that life are a thousand times better than the best days in this life. This belief is at the heart of the Pascal Mystery. As Catholics we believe that receiving the Eucharist enters us into the Pascal Mystery. Likewise, the sacrament of Anointing of the Sick with Viaticum is intended to be preparation for the journey home.

---

130. Charles J. Healey, *Christian Spirituality: An Introduction to the Heritage* (New York: Alba, 1999), 402-403.

The sacraments of Baptism, Matrimony, Holy Orders, Anointing and, in some cases, Confirmation, come to us at the apex of many of life's major transitions. They are meant to make visible the invisible reality that God is with us and loves us during times of transition and change, even when we do not feel God's presence.

Likewise, the sacraments of Eucharist and Penance are intended, in part, to sustain us during times of trial, such as when we are struggling with change. For "The partaking of the Body and Blood of Christ has no less an effect than to change us into what we have received."[131]

The relationship between continuity and change is not that they are opposites, but that they complement each other. This is reflected in the Eucharist when the bread and wine are changed into the body and blood of Christ. Outwardly the host remains the same, but theologically its substance has changed.

The sacraments not only reflect change, the lot of being human; they also have changed significantly since Vatican II. In our own day, the rites for the celebration of the Eucharist have been changed in many and important ways, bringing them more into line with modern spiritual and psychological needs.[132] This is one of the comments from Vatican II regarding change and the sacraments:

> For the liturgy is made up of unchangeable elements divinely instituted, and of elements subject to change. These latter not only may be changed but ought to be changed with the passage of time, if they have suffered from the intrusion of anything out of harmony with the inner nature of the liturgy or have become less suitable.[133]

We need to have sacraments or sacred spaces in our lives to help us adjust to change. These sacred spaces, however, need not be reserved to churches, temples and synagogues, and those who perform the sacred rituals need not be restricted to the clergy. As Haughton suggests, we need to recognize the permeability of the membrane that separates this world from the sacred.[134] God is revealed in the every day changeable events of life. Anything (and anyone) can be sacramental, ultimately because God loved it into being.[135]

---

131. *Instruction on the Worship of the Eucharistic Mystery*, S.C.R., *Eucharisticum Mysterium*, 25 May, 1967. & *Constitution on the Church*, n. 26: *AAS* 57 (1965), pp. 31–32.

132. *Instruction on the Manner of Distributing Holy Communion*, S.C.D.W. *Memoriale Domini*, (29 May, 1969).

133. *The Constitution on the Sacred Liturgy*, Vatican II, *Sacrosanctum Concilium* (4 December, 1963), #21.

134. Haughton, 128.

135. Livingston, 41.

In this chapter we have examined the three primary sources for our spirituality during times of change: Scripture, tradition and sacraments. These can be thought of as different melodies that can guide our dance with change. While we have been able to scratch only the surface in these three areas, clearly they offer us an ever ready reservoir of material from which to draw our spiritual tools for adapting to changes in the Church.

Chapter 5—
A Spiritual Path Through
Change—The LEAP of Faith

Introduction

To choose a spiritual path for adapting to changes in the Church can put us on a road less traveled.[136] There are almost as many spiritual paths through change as there are people. We find certain aspects of spirituality that resonate with us and others that do not. What will be advanced here is one spiritual framework for adapting to changes in the Church entitled, *The LEAP of Faith.* LEAP is an acronym for four of the five major spiritual components of this method designed for dealing with changes in the Church: Learning, Experience, Action and Prayer.[137]

Foundation

A necessary precondition for employing this spiritual method is to focus on self. In confronting any of life's problems, we readily see the shortcomings of others. The problem is always caused by someone else. Because the problem is out there, it is always others who need to change.[138]

The premise of this spiritual path is to accept and adapt to changes in the Church, not to fight them. When it comes to difficulty in dealing with changes, the problem is not out there, but inside each one of us. The external system that we often complain about actually exists within each of us. We continually propagate and preserve the structures of the various systems by our daily behavior.[139] For this spiritual approach to changes in the Church, then, to have any beneficial effect, we must keep the focus on ourselves.

---

136. Borrowing the title from a poem by Robert Frost.
137. The acronym LEAP was devised by this writer and Rev. Douglas DellaPietra.
138. Quinn, 32-33.
139. Ibid., 101.

Elements

Learning

Learning is an important ingredient and a spiritual principle for adapting to changes in the Church. What we must learn about primarily is our usual reaction to change in general and then to change in the Church specifically. Information must actively be sought from everywhere, from places and sources we never before thought to consult. The intent of this new information is to keep us a little off balance, alert to how we might need to change. Spiritually mature individuals do not look for information that makes them feel good, or that verifies their past and validates their present. They deliberately look for information that might threaten their stability, unbalance them, and open them to growth and further learning.[140]

The learning and information we seek is a dynamic, changing element. Without information, life cannot give birth to anything new; information, especially about ourselves, is absolutely essential for beginning to adapt well to the changes going on in the Church.

We must develop greater self-knowledge. We must have a clear idea of our core identity and the identity of our Church. Is our identity tied to the Sunday 11:30 A.M. Mass at St. Mary's Church or is our identity rooted in the deep, rich, productive soil of faith in Jesus Christ, the Risen Lord? The former identity would be much more fragile than the latter. Is our parish Church's identity tied to surviving at all costs, or can we enter into the Paschal Mystery which is proclaimed every time we celebrate the Holy Mass? In order to adapt well to change, people need to be connected to the fundamental identity of their community.[141]

We need to learn about the process of change in general. What are the reasons people resist change? What are some of the emotions we can expect to feel as we are going through change? Do these emotions hold up to the light of scrutiny? We may feel that some change is threatening our identity, but feelings are not facts.[142] Sometimes when we examine our feelings in light of reality, we find that the feelings are baseless or have a basis in something other than the immediate change to which we are trying to adapt.

We need to learn about how others, especially those we hold in high regard, deal effectively with Church changes (and any of the spiritual methods they may

---

140. Wheatley, 83.

141. Ibid., 146.

142. Borrowing a phrase from a dear friend, Dr. Elaine Yudashkin.

employ). Not all methods will necessarily work for all of us; however, some unique method utilized by another might be exactly what we need for coping.

We also need to learn all that we can about the proposed change with which we are dealing. Too many people make crucial decisions about change on the basis of incomplete and biased information. Sometimes, when all the facts are known, what initially appeared to be a "bad" change can turn out to be a most advantageous change. We need to resist our instinctively negative reaction to change (which often causes us to close our minds to the truth), and ask many questions about the proposed change until all available information is obtained.

We must try to engage nonlinear thinking and intuition, and access alternative forms of expressions such as drama, art, stories, and pictures. A critical task of learning is to evoke all of our senses, not just our gray matter.[143]

Finally, we need to discover and develop metaphors that will help us to see change in a different light (e.g., instead of the thought that information is power, we begin to think of information as nourishment for the soul). This shift will keep our attention on the fact that information is essential for dealing with change, as essential as the food we eat.

Experience

Change evokes a range of feelings. It is common when dealing with change to experience feelings of loss and grief. As we discussed earlier, the first stage of change involves a death of something. We need to grieve over our losses or else they will begin to accumulate and we will pay a higher price later for ignoring our grief now. The quickest and most effective way for resolving our feelings is to experience and honor them.

In adapting to changes in the Church, we need to acknowledge that something is dying. The acknowledgment may be elaborate (a liturgy or ritual of some kind) or it may simply come in conversation with others experiencing the same changes. Too often, when people are reluctant to move on, we call it resistance when it may be a grieving process. Any attempt to rush past grieving and the sense of loss will (ironically) slow the process down.[144]

Genuine changes often entail suffering, the experience at times of being physically ripped apart where the ultimate outcome is in doubt—real doubt. What endures in the face of this is the spirit that gave rise to the effort in the first place. What is common in all stories of transformation is the experience of dying and then beginning again, the Paschal Mystery.[145]

---

143. Wheatley, 143.
144. Peter Block, *Flawless Consulting* (San Francisco: Jossey-Bass, 1981), 196.
145. Ibid., 197.

We also need to examine our feelings in the light of day. Here are some questions we can ask ourselves which may help us to get a better handle on our feelings:

- What is a current situation in which you are having difficulty dealing with change?
- When you look at the change, what thoughts, feelings, and emotions surface for you?
- Often what arises for us with change is a sense of fear. Can you identify any fear you have/had about this change?
- Are there any obstacles/barriers you have encountered in yourself or others concerning the change?
- Do you find that your initial reaction to the change is your usual reaction to most changes you encounter?
- What would you do differently—the way you do your work or live your life—if you were completely unafraid? How would this change your situation?

Examining our feelings about change can sometimes cause a complete shift in perspective and a reversal of the way we feel, since, as was mentioned previously, feelings are not facts.

Experiencing change means living in the moment. Being present in the moment does not mean that we act without intention or flow directionless through life without any plans. But we would do better to attend more carefully to the process by which we create our plans and intentions. Healthy processes create better relationships among us, more clarity about who we are, and more information about what is going on around us. With these new connections, we grow healthier. We develop greater capacity to know what to do. We weave together a support system that is as resilient and flexible as a building designed to withstand earthquakes.[146]

The lesson to be learned from those who have successfully dealt with changes in the Church is that the change process goes through a series of phases that usually requires considerable time. Skipping necessary steps creates only the illusion of speed and seldom produces a satisfying result.[147]

Action

Change means surrendering control and yet, paradoxically, by employing spiritual principles, we can regain some measure of control (at the very least, over our

---

146. Wheatley, 155.
147. Jay Alden Conger, et al eds. *The Leader's Change Handbook: An Essential Guide to Setting Direction and Taking Action* (San Francisco: Jossey-Bass, 1998), 87.

reaction to change). There is a difference between managing change and embracing change. When we only manage change, we wait until we are told to change, and then we comply minimally and halfheartedly. Embracing change means we actively look for some positive action to take which cooperates with or furthers the change. By doing so, we are becoming a change agent, rather than a victim of change.

Action is in some ways an extension of learning, since it fosters learning by doing instead of reading, hearing, or thinking. During the change process, our internal self can get out of alignment with our external world. One way to realign the self is to retell the most important stories that are connected with that which is being changed. We go through the ritual of telling some core stories that are very central to our identity. When we repeat these stories, we do not ever retell them exactly. We recount them from the perspective of the current change we are dealing with in the Church. What we are really doing is realigning our past to include our present and future.

The action could also be dividing the change into smaller, more acceptable pieces. We must let go of the need to accept immediately the entirety of the change. Instead, we can work toward finding meaning and personal energy in one area of the change. If we succeed in generating passion in one area, our internal resistance to the change may diminish.

When we take intelligent and meaningful risks, they leave us with a sense of empowerment.[148] This, in turn, can lead to a greater sense of meaning, competence, self-determination and impact. Instead of being passive victims of change, we play a part in influencing and shaping the change.

Prayer

In 1943, Reinhold Neibuhr composed what could conceivably be THE perfect mantra for those going through change. Known as the Serenity Prayer, it is used extensively by those in Twelve Step programs.

> God, grant me the serenity
> to accept the things I cannot change,
> the courage to change the things I can
> and the wisdom to know the difference.[149]

Paradoxically, one of the things we cannot change is change. What we can change is our reaction to change. This can be accomplished through the power of prayer.

---

148. Quinn, 226-27.
149. Reinhold Neibuhr, 1943.

In fact, prayer not only impacts our acceptance of change; our acceptance of change can also be reflected in our prayer. Harkening back to our previous consideration of good change vs. bad change vs. inevitable change in Chapter One, there is an extraordinary example of how someone employed her spiritual tools and principles in order to deal in a prayerful way with what all would agree was a bad change. This prayer was found next to the body of a dead child when the World War II concentration camp at Ravensbrook was liberated:

O God, remember not only the women and men of good will. But also those of ill will.

But do not only remember the suffering they have inflicted on us, remember the fruits we brought thanks to this suffering: our comradeship, our loyalty, our humility, the courage, the generosity, the greatness of heart that has grown out of all of this.

And when they come to judgment, let all the fruits we have bourne be for their forgiveness. Amen. Amen. Amen.[150]

Inviting the Holy Spirit to be with and guide us in the ways of adapting to change through prayer is absolutely essential. We can ask the Holy Spirit for enlightenment, helping us to discern what positive elements God might be bringing forth from the change.

The following prayer by Thomas Merton is also a good prayer to employ during times of change:

MY LORD GOD, I have no idea where I am going. I do not see the road ahead of me. I cannot know for certain where it will end. Nor do I really know myself, and the fact that I think that I am following your will does not mean that I am actually doing so. But I believe that the desire to please you does in fact please you. And I hope I have that desire in all that I am doing. I hope that I will never do anything apart from that desire. And I know that if I do this you will lead me by the right road though I may know nothing about it. Therefore will I trust you always though I may seem to be lost and in the shadow of death. I will not fear, for you are ever with me, and you will never leave me to face my perils alone.[151]

In prayer, the Holy Spirit is given the time and the opportunity to touch the hearts of those struggling with change, to let them know that, no matter what, they will never be left alone as they struggle through the changes that life throws

---

150. Nassal, 75.
151. Thomas Merton, *Thoughts in Solitude* (London: Burns & Oates, 1975), 126.

at them. Nevertheless, in spite of such assurances, all people facing change must ultimately take a LEAP of faith, trusting that in the end all will be well and that all is in accord with a plan set out before the dawning of time.

Faith

The last component of our model for a spirituality that will sustain us during times of change in the Church is faith. Faith is not an act of understanding, it is an act of the will: a decision to trust in the promises of God despite doubts and disappointments. Faith also connects the believer to Christ. Nevertheless, faith can come into conflict with reason and experience. To be Christian is to decide to plunge into a world of darkness devoid of proof, reason, or experience. Doubt and uncertainty create opportunities for the renewed act of the will to have faith. Faith ultimately rests on the certainty and power of God rather than on our own power and certainty. The Psalms abound with examples of struggles with doubt, uncertainty and anxiety. Ultimately, we need to have faith that the same God who raised Jesus from the dead will give us all that we need to adapt, and adapt well, to the changes going on in the Church, now and in the years to come.

Praxis

This book has its roots in a three-year evaluation, conducted by this writer, of the pastoral planning process employed the Roman Catholic Diocese of Rochester. At the end of that evaluation there were several recommendations issued for the future. This was one of those recommendations:

> This writer was saddened and disturbed by a propensity which mani-fested itself in many meetings, side discussions, and qualitative survey comments. This tendency could best be described as an extension of the NIMBY (Not in My Back Yard) mentality so prevalent in secular society today. The reasoning goes like this, "Yes, I understand that we have fewer priests, and yes I understand that some Churches are going to have to close as a result, BUT NOT MY CHURCH!" It is so sad to see this operative in the Church, since it betrays a complete lack of understanding and commitment to the self sacrifice which Christ demonstrated in his life and to which he calls us as his followers. Therefore, it would appear that some very well thought out catechesis should precede the next entry into the pastoral planning process.[152]

---

152. Richard McCorry, *User Satisfaction Survey of the Pastoral Planning Process of the Roman Catholic Diocese of Rochester, New York* (Unpublished Thesis, April 13, 1999).

Taking up this challenge, Rev. Douglas DellaPietra, a Roman Catholic priest of the Rochester Diocese, and this writer created and conducted experiential reflection sessions designed to give participants some spiritual tools to help them adapt to changes in the Church. These reflection sessions were done under the auspices of the Pastoral Planning department of the Diocese of Rochester, NY.

The reflection sessions were designed around the metaphor of 'LEAP.' Not only was it the spiritual metaphor promoted at the reflection sessions; it was also the model for the four major components to the reflection sessions given. These four components, although not presented in this order, are:

1. Learning.
2. Experiential
3. Action
4. Prayer

By design, there was a small learning component to these presentations. This element was small because most of the struggles people have around change occur on the feeling level and not on the intellectual level. Nevertheless, participants were invited to consider the implications of the story of the disciples on the road to Emmaus for their own lived circumstances of change. They were also introduced to the metaphor of "stumbling in the light,"[153] and encouraged to weigh its implications for dealing with change.

Since most of the struggles people have around change transpire on the feelings level, by far the largest component of these reflection sessions was experiential, both individually and in small groups. In terms of the individual experiential component, participants were given handouts that contained questions along with space for the participant's responses. Initially, participants were asked to respond in writing to the questions listed on page 59.

In order to establish the ground rules for the small group work, people were asked to honor the confidentiality of what people would share. Furthermore, participants were instructed that when they broke into their small groups, they were to listen to what the others shared and not to offer advice or feedback. With that, participants were divided into groups of three or four and asked to share their responses to the previous questions. One of the things that was learned along the way was that people should be informed ahead of time that they would be asked to share their responses in small groups. This was based upon feedback from participants in an earlier reflection session that they had initially chosen a very personal change issue and then had to scramble for something less personal when

---

153. Kysar.

informed that they would be sharing this in small groups. After the participants had viewed the video version of *Who Moved My Cheese*,[154] they were asked to reflect and write on the following question: "What can you use from the story to apply to your situation?" Again, the participants went into their small groups to share their responses to this question with the others. Recollecting one of the questions posed in the video version of *Who Moved My Cheese*, participants were also asked to reflect and write a response to the following questions: "What would you do differently—the way you do your work or live your life—if you were completely unafraid? How would this change your situation?"

The prayer component was woven throughout the presentation. After the introduction of the presenters and participants, there was an opening prayer, inviting the Holy Spirit to guide the participants in the ways of adapting to change. The final prayer experience began with a prayer to the Holy Spirit asking for enlightenment, as those attending were then invited to reflect on the last question, "What might God be bringing forth from this change which is positive?" After some time to think and write a response to this question, Thomas Merton's prayer from *Thoughts in Solitude* was read. This was immediately followed with a singing of the 62nd psalm according to the rendition of John Michael Talbot. This song concluded the reflection session.

Finally, the action component of the reflection session was the charge given to participants. They were commissioned to put into action the concepts and strategies presented at the reflection session. Furthermore, they were encouraged to go out and share this material with someone else within the next 24 hours, if they were interested in solidifying the material in their own mind. Fully half of the total time of the reflection session was devoted to the experiential and prayerful components of the reflection session. This was intentionally done so that the Holy Spirit might have ample time to touch the hearts of the participants to let them know that no matter what, they will never be left alone as they struggle through the changes that life throws at them. Nevertheless, in spite of such assurances, the participants, and all people facing change, must ultimately take a LEAP of faith, trusting that all will be well.

The first reflection session given was in conjunction with a diocesan Leadership Training day. Those attending were primarily parish lay pastoral leaders, although it was open to priests and to diocesan leaders as well. Subsequent reflection sessions have been given to both staffs and parishioners of urban, suburban, and rural parishes of all sizes. Over the past two years, approximately twenty-one reflection sessions have been given in all. Many have offered their feedback (on a participant evaluation form after the reflection sessions were completed).

---

154. Spencer Johnson, *Who Moved My Cheese* (New York: Putnam, 2000).

Feedback

It would be fair to say, based upon responses given to a survey conducted at the end of these reflection sessions, that the average participant came into the reflection session feeling somewhat comfortable with changes in the Church. Participants were then asked to report how comfortable they felt with change in the Church after attending the reflection session. Overall, there was a positive shift in the participants' disposition toward change in the Church after experiencing these reflection sessions. Interestingly, even those who reported feeling less comfortable with changes in the Church after attending these reflection sessions would still recommend this reflection session to others. This would indicate that there were factors operative within these people, other than their satisfaction with the reflection session, which were causing them to feel less comfortable with change after coming to these presentations.

Almost all participants felt that this material had applicability to changes in their life besides changes in the Church. All participants commented that they would like similar reflection sessions to be put on in the future. Almost all of the participants reported that they would recommend this reflection session to others. At the same time most felt that they were leaving these reflection sessions better equipped to help others see changes in the Church differently, presumably in a more positive way. Finally, all of the participants reported that they felt they had learned ways to see the presence of God in the midst of transition and change. As a result of the positive experience of these reflection sessions that many people have reported, the Diocese of Rochester is now highly recommending these reflection sessions to those involved in parish councils as well as parish and diocesan pastoral planning.

Participant evaluations such as these are heartening and have encouraged Fr. DellaPietra and this writer that they are on the right track. Nevertheless, both sense that these reflection sessions have only scratched the surface of the available material that might enhance these reflection sessions and the ultimate goal of helping the participants find spiritual strength in the midst of change.

One Person's Experience

Susan is a 39 year old, married white female. She has three children, all still living at home. She earned a Master in Theology degree from St. Bernard's School of Theology and Ministry. She has been employed as a director of religious education for the past two years in a medium sized, suburban Roman Catholic parish. Prior to that, she was a coordinator for religious education for four years in the same parish. She has also worked as a public school teacher. Susan attended two of the "LEAP of Faith" reflection sessions and was in a unique position to offer her feedback on this experience.

Drawing upon the image of a new pair of shoes, Susan said that she likes change and sees it as an opportunity, as long as she has the chance to process it, just as it takes a bit of time to break in new shoes.

> Everything's a change, but it's new. You know, it's new. There's nothing wrong with new. It's just uncomfortable. It's like a pair of shoes. Talk to anyone, you know, who has a fetish for shoes. You don't wear them the first time and have them be comfortable. You've got to break them in.[155]

She explained that to process change means to have sufficient time as well as a support group with which to talk. Time reduces resistance to change both for her and for others whom she has observed. Her approach to change is to engage it.

Change in the Church is good, according to Susan. It presents challenges and opportunities, and Susan believes that only good can come from it. She believes that we have a responsibility, when faced with change, to work with it rather than to resist it. Spiritually, Susan approaches and processes change with prayer, educating herself about the change, time in silence, gathering with others to process the change, and considering change with an open mind and heart.

Overall, she enjoyed attending the LEAP of Faith reflection sessions. Susan especially liked the reflective questions and small group work. She also liked beginning and ending with prayer. She also provided a constructive observation: she would have liked more time in small groups and wished there had been more large group sharing.

> I would have liked a little more time to have those small group discussions and then hear more from the larger group. That would probably be my only criticism of the whole program, because I thought that those were excellent questions and the process was wonderful. It was really set up well.[156]

There is no single approach which will slay the "change dragon." There is no magic formula that will help people breeze through the changes that are in the Church's future. After entering into a dialog about change, and wrestling with the "change dragon" for a while, what we are left with is the requirement to take a LEAP of faith. To LEAP over the moat in which the "change dragon" hides:

- Into the arms of a loving Father who journeys with us through turbulent times of change

---

155. Taken from a transcription of a taped interview between "Susan" and this writer. (Fall, 2002).
156. Ibid.

- Into the arms of our Savior who tells us over and over again in Scripture, "Be not afraid."
- Into the Spirit of God who, we know by faith, continues to guide our Church into the perfection which will ultimately bring about God's kingdom here on Earth.

It is this LEAP of faith that will sustain us and give us courage to face a future filled with change.

Conclusion

Change in the Church can be hell for some. Yet not to change, to stay on the path of slow death, is also hell. Change in the Church can also be heaven, both metaphorically and actually. Which perception becomes dominant depends primarily on our disposition toward change. The hell of deep change is the hero's journey.[157] This spiritual journey puts us on a path of exhilaration, growth and progress. In adapting to change in the Church, we become aligned and revitalized because we are cooperating with life on life's terms. Properly disposed, we can find the vision to empower both ourselves and our faith communities.[158]

Change in the Church will not change, but we can. Church changes will always be with us, and it will be our job to transition through them. These times of transition will not be easy, and yet change can be a positive force in our lives, especially in the lives of those in the Church, and could turn us to new and wonderful directions. It can help us to become the type of Church we have always wanted to be, or more importantly, the type of Church God wishes us to be. A lot depends on us. We can see change as threat or as possibility, danger or invitation, problem or opportunity. The way we see it is how we will relate to it, since perception plays a large role in how we view reality. The choice is ours. We may have to surrender some of our illusions, while not giving up our convictions or dreams. Changes and transitions in the Church offer us much. They offer us the possibility of building up the perfect body of Christ right here on Earth: dancing our way gracefully and joyfully into a future filled with exciting change, bringing us ever closer to the kingdom of God.

---

157. Quinn, 126.
158. Ibid., 78 & 79.

Bibliography

By Subject Area

1. Organizational Change Management Strategies

a. *Books*

Anderson, Leith. *Dying for Change*. Minneapolis: Bethany House Publishers, 1990.

Argyris, Chris. *Knowledge for Action: a Guide to Overcoming Barriers to Organizational Change*. San Francisco: Jossey-Bass, 1993.

Baum, David H. *Lightning in a Bottle: Proven Lessons for Leading Change*. Chicago: Dearborn, 2000.

Berger, Lance A. and Martin J. Sikora, with Dorothy R. Berger. *Change Management Handbook: a Road Map to Corporate Transformation*. Burr Ridge: Irwin Professional Publication, 1994.

Block, Peter. *The Flawless Consulting Fieldbook and Companion*. San Francisco: Jossey-Bass, 1981.

Bridges, William. *Managing Transitions: Making the Most of Change*. Reading: Addison-Wesley, 1991.

Champy, James and Nitin Nohria. *Fast Forward: The Best Ideas on Managing Business Change*. Boston: Harvard Business School Publication, 1996.

Conger, Jay Alden et al eds. *The Leader's Change Handbook: An Essential Guide to Setting Direction and Taking Action*. San Francisco: Jossey-Bass, 1998.

Heifetz, Ronald A. *Leadership Without Easy Answers*. Cambridge, MA: Belknap, 1994.

Johnson, Spencer. *Who Moved My Cheese*. New York: Putnam, 2000.

Keener, James O. B. *10 Good Reasons Why People Resist Change: and Practical Strategies That Win the Day*. Cleveland: Grand River Publications, 1999.

Kegan, Robert and Lisa Lahey. *How the Way We Talk Can Change the Way We Work: Seven Languages for Transformation*. San Francisco: Jossey-Bass, 2001.

Kotter, John. *Leading Change*. Boston: Harvard Business School Press, 1996.

Kotter, John P. and Dan S. Cohen. *The Heart of Change: Real-Life Stories of How People Change Their Organizations*. Boston: Harvard Business School Press, 2002.

Miller, William R. and Stephen Rollnick. *Motivational Interviewing: Preparing People for Change.* New York: Guilford, 2002.

Nadler, David. *Champions of Change: How CEOS and Their Companies Are Mastering the Skills of Radical Change.* San Francisco: Jossey-Bass, 1998.

O'Toole, James. *Leading Change: Overcoming the Ideology of Comfort and the Tyranny of Custom.* San Francisco: Jossey-Bass Publishers, 1995.

Quinn, Robert. *Deep Change: Discovering the Leader Within.* San Francisco: Jossey-Bass., 1996.

Winters, Mary-Frances. *Only Wet Babies Like Change: Workplace Wisdom for Baby Boomers.* Chantilly: Renaissance Books, 2002.

b. *Articles*

Agocs, Carol. "Institutionalized Resistance to Organizational Change: Denial, Inaction and Repression." *Journal of Business Ethics 16 #* 9, 917-931.

Axley, S. "Communicating Change: Questions to Consider." *Industrial Management 42* #4, 18-22.

Beer, Michael R., A. Eisenstat and Bert Spector. "Why Change Programs Don't Produce Change." *Harvard Business Review.* November-December 1990.

Bernardez, Mariano L. "Start Small, Change Big." *Management Review,* June 1997, 21.

Cripe, Edward J. "Use Graphic Metaphors to Communicate Organizational Change." *Communication World 14* #1, 34.

Finnie, Bill and Marilyn Norris. "On Leading Change: a Conversation with John P. Kotter." *Strategy & Leadership 25* #1, 1997, 18.

Goodstein, L. and W. Burke. "Creating Successful Organizational Change," *Organizational Dynamics 19* #4, 5-17.

Kotter, John P. "Leading Change: Why Transformation Efforts Fail." *Harvard Business Review 73* #2, 59-67.

Larkin, T. and S. Larkin. "Reaching & Changing Frontline Employees." *Harvard Business Review 74* #3, 95-104.

Mann, D. "Why Supervisors Resist Change & What You Can Do About It." *Journal for Quality & Participation 23* #3, 20-22.

Pascale, Richard, Mark Millemann and Linda Gioja. "Changing the Way We Change." *Harvard Business Review 75* #6, 86.

Sanchez, Paul. "Agents for Change." *Communication World 14* #3, 52.

Schneider, Benjamin, Arthur P. Brief and Richard A. Guzzo. "Creating Climate and Culture for Sustainable Organizational Change." *Organizational Dynamics 24* #4, 6.

Strebel, P. "Why Do Employees Resist Change?" *Harvard Business Review 74* #3, 86-92.

"How Change Really Happens," *Training 37* #10, 122-126.

2. Spirituality and Change

a. *Books*

Arbuckle, Gerald. *Change, Grief, and Renewal in the Church: a Spirituality for a New Era.* Westminster: Christian Classics, 1991.

Berneking, Nancy J. and Pamela Carter, ed. *Re-Membering and Re-Imagining.* Cleveland: Pilgrim Press, 1995.

Bireley, Robert. *The Refashioning of Catholicism, 1450-1700. A Reassessment of the Counter Reformation.* Washington, D.C: The Catholic University of America Press, 1999.

Brumet, Robert. *Finding Yourself in Transition: Using Life's Changes for Spiritual Awakening.* Unity Village: Unity Books, 1995.

Fleck, J. Roland and John D. Carter. *Psychology and Christianity: Integrative Readings.* Nashville: Abingdon, 1981.

Ford, Leighton. *Transforming Leadership: Jesus' Way of Creating Vision, Shaping Values and Empowering Change.* Downers Grove: InterVarsity Press, 1993.

Haughton, Rosemary Luling. *Images for Change: The Transformation of Society.* New York: Paulist Press, 1997.

Hauser, Richard J. *Finding God in Troubled Times: The Holy Spirit and Suffering.* New York: Paulist, 1994.

Healey, Charles J. *Christian Spirituality: An Introduction to the Heritage.* New York: Alba, 1999.

Herrington, Jim, Mike Bonem, James H. Furr. *Leading Congregational Change: A Practical Guide for the Transformational Journey.* San Francisco: Jossey-Bass, 2000.

Holmes, Urban T. *A History of Christian Spirituality, An Analytical Introduction.* New York: The Seabury Press, 1980.

Kraft, William F. *Ways of the Desert: Becoming Holy Through Difficult Times.* New York: Haworth, 2000.

Kysar, Robert. *Stumbling in the Light: New Testament Images for a Changing Church.* St. Louis: Chalice Press, 1999.

La Chapelle, David. *Navigating the Tides of Change: Stories from Science, the Sacred, and a Wise Planet.* British Columbia: New Society Publishers, 2001.

Lee, Jung Young. *The Theology of Change: A Christian Concept of God in an Eastern Perspective.* Maryknoll: Orbis, 1979.

Lee, Jung Young. *Embracing Change: Postmodern Interpretations of the I Ching from a Christian Perspective.* Scranton: University of Scranton Press, 1994.

Livingston, Patricia H. *Lessons of the Heart: Celebrating the Rhythms of Life.* Notre Dame: Ave Maria Press, 1992.

Long, Jr., Edward Leroy and Robert T. Handy. *Theology and Church in Times of Change.* Philadelphia: Westminster Press, 1970.

Maalouf, Amin. *In the Name of Identity: Violence and the Need to Belong.* New York: Arcade, 2001.

McGrath, Alister E. *Spirituality in an Age of Change: Rediscovering the Spirit of the Reformers.* Grand Rapids: Zondervan, 1994.

Meister, Michael F. *Challenged by Change: Perceptions and Perspectives.* Romeoville: Christian Brothers Publications, 1991.

Merton, Thomas. *Thoughts in Solitude.* London: Burns & Oates, 1975.

Miller, William R. *Living As If: How Positive Faith Can Change Your Life* Philadelphia: Westminster Press, 1985.

Miller, William R. and John E. Martin eds. *Behavior Therapy and Religion: Integrating Spiritual And Behavioral Approaches to Change.* Newbury Park: Sage Publications, 1988.

Mitchell, Kenneth R. and Herbert Anderson. *All Our Losses, All Our Griefs: Resources For Pastoral Care.* Philadelphia: Westminister, 1983.

Nelson, Alan. *How to Change Your Church Without Killing It.* Nashville: West Publishing, 2000.

Newman, Cardinal J. H. *An Essay on the Development of Doctrine.* London: Longmans, 1845.

Pope John XXIII's address on the occasion of the opening of the Second Vatican Council, October 11, 1962.

Rolheiser, Ronald. *The Holy Longing: The Search for a Christian Spirituality.* New York: Doubleday, 1999.

Rupp, Joyce. *Praying Our Goodbyes.* Notre Dame: Ave Maria, 1988.

Sweet, Leonard I. ed. *Communication and Change in American Religious History.* Grand Rapids: Eerdmans, 1993.

Tacey, David J. *Remaking Men: Jung, Spirituality and Social Change.* New York: Routledge, 1997.

Watley, William D. *You Have to Face it to Fix it: Sermons on the Challenges of Life.* Valley Forge: Judson Press, 1997.

Wilhelm, Hellmut. *Change: Eight Lectures on the I Ching.* Princeton: Princeton University Press, 1973.

b. *Articles*

Ammerman, Nancy Tatom. "Congregations In The Midst Of Change: An Interview," *Christian Century,* 114 (Jan. 15, 1997), 48-51.

Bento, Regina F. "The Little Inn at the Crossroads: A Spiritual Approach to the Design of a Leadership Course." *Journal of Management Education,* 24 #5, 650-661.

Craft, Carolyn M. "Spirituality for Passionate and Rapidly Changing Times." *Cross Currents,* (Winter, 1996-1997), 539-544.

Deschenes, Paul and Martha L. Rogers. "A Systems View of Jesus as Change Agent." *Journal of Psychology & Theology,* 9 (Summer, 1981),128-135.

Jeffrey, George J. "In change, Unchanged." *Expository Times,* 62, 55-56.

Kraybill, J. Nelson. "Power and Authority: Helping the Church Face Problems and Adapt to Change." *Conrad Grebel Review,* 17, 17-34.

Labowitz, Shoni. "Spirituality as a Powerful Force of Change." *Tikkun,* 13, 62-63.

Preston, Ronald H. "Reflections on Theologies of Social Change." In *Theology and Change: Essays in Memory of Alan Richardson.* London: S C M Press, 1975.

Propst, L. Rebecca. "A Comparison of the Cognitive Restructuring Psychotherapy Paradigm and Several Spiritual Approaches to Mental Health." *Journal of Psychology and Theology,* (Summer 1980), 107-114.

Qualls, Paula Fontana. "Mark 11:15-18: A Prophetic Challenge." *Review & Expositor,* 93 (Summer, 1999), 395-402.

Shepperson, Vance L. "Paradox, Parables, and Change: One Approach to Christian Hypnotherapy." *Journal of Psychology & Theology,* 9, 3-11.

Sofield, Loughlan and Rosine Hammett. "Experiencing Termination in Community." *Human Development*, 2 #2, 24-31.

Tucker, Joyce C. "Challenge amid Change: The Call to Church Leadership." *The Princeton Seminary Bulletin*, 15 #3, 241.

"Out with the Old, in with the New," *Canada and the World Backgrounder*, (May 1998), 28-31.

c. *Recordings*

Padovano, Anthony. "Spirituality in a Time of Change," *Audio Theology Digest*, 1974. Sound Recording.

Miller, James. *Nothing is Permanent Except Change*. Fort Wayne: Willowgreen, 1991. Videotape.

3. Prophecy

Blenkinsopp, Joseph. *Sage, Priest and Prophet: Religious and Intellectual Leadership in Ancient Israel*. Louisville: Westminster John Knox, 1995.

Carroll, Robert P. *From Chaos to Covenant: Prophecy in the Book of Jeremiah*. New York: Crossroad, 1981.

Dube, Musa. *Postcolonial Feminist Interpretation of the Bible*. St. Louis: Chalice Press, 2000.

Fettke, Steven M. *Messages to a Nation in Crisis: an Introduction to the Prophecy of Jeremiah*. Washington, D.C.: University Press of America, 1983.

Fiorenza, Elisabeth Schussler. *In Memory of Her*. New York: Crossroad, 1983.

Franklin, Robert. *Liberating Visions: Human Fulfillment and Social Justice in African American Thought*. Minneapolis: Fortress, 1990.

Gowan, Donald E. *Theology of the Prophetic Books: the Death and Resurrection of Israel*. Louisville: Westminster John Knox Press, 1998.

Herzog, William R., II. *Prophecy in Israel and Judah*. Class Handout, 2002.

Herzog, William R., II. *Jesus, Justice and the Reign of God*. Louisville: Westminster John Knox, 2000.

Horsley, Richard A. *Hearing the Whole Story: the Politics of Plot in Mark's Gospel*. Louisville: Westminster John Knox Press, 2001.

Horsley, Richard and John Hanson. *Bandits, Prophets and Messiahs: Popular Movements at the Time of Jesus*. Harrisburg, PA: Trinity Press International, 1985.

Kidner, Derek. *The Message of Jeremiah: Against Wind and Tide,* Downers Grove: Inter-Varsity Press, 1987.

Lemke, Werner E. "The Prophets in a Time of Crisis," *Covenant Quarterly,* 27 #3, August 1969.

Wilson, Robert R. *Prophecy and Society in Ancient Israel.* Minneapolis: Fortress, 1984.

Wink, Walter. *Engaging the Powers: Discernment and Resistance in a World of Domination.* Minneapolis: Fortress, 1992.

4. Conflict Resolution in Faith Communities

Brown, Raymond E. and John P. Meier. *Antioch and Rome: New Testament Cradles of Catholic Christianity.* New York: Paulist Press, 1983.

Carter, Jay. *Nasty People.* Columbus: McGraw Hill, 1989.

Couture, Pamela D. and Rodney J. Hunter ed. *Pastoral Care and Social Conflict.* Nashville: Abingdon Press, 1995.

Goodstein, Leonard D., Bernard Lubin, Alice W. Lubin ed. *Cases in Conflict Management.* La Jolla: University Associates, 1979.

Kolb, Deborah M. and Jean M. Bartunek, ed. *Hidden Conflict in Organizations: Uncovering Behind-the-scenes Disputes.* Newbury Park: Sage Publications, 1992.

Kraybill, Ronald S. *Peace Skills: Manual for Community Mediators.* San Francisco: Jossey-Bass, 2001.

Nassal, Joseph. *Premeditated Mercy a Spirituality of Reconciliation.* Leavenworth: Forest of Peace Books, 2000.

Ragsdale, Katherine Hancock. *Boundary Wars.* Cleveland: Pilgrim Press, 1996.

Rediger, Lloyd. *Clergy Killers: Guidance for Pastors and Congregations under Attack.* Louisville: Westminster John Knox Press, 1997.

Sofield, Loughlan, Rosine Hammett and Carroll Juliano, *Building Community: Christian, Caring, Vital.* Notre Dame: Ave Maria Press, 1998.

Sofield, Loughlan and Carroll Juliano. *Collaborative Ministry: Skills and Guidelines.* Notre Dame: Ave Maria Press, 1987.

Sofield, Loughlan, Rosine Hammett and Carroll Juliano. *Design for Wholeness: Dealing with Anger, Learning to Forgive, Building Self-Esteem.* Notre Dame: Ave Maria Press, 1990.

Willimon, William, *Preaching about Conflict in The Local Church.* Philadelphia: Westminster Press, 1987.

MSNBC News Story "Judge Rules Renovations at Sacred Heart Can Continue," August 28, 2003, <http://www.msnbc.com/local/whec/M8610.asp>.

About the Author

Dr. Richard J. McCorry is the senior ministry associate at St. Pius Tenth Church in Rochester, NY, a large suburban parish of approximately 2300 registered families. Prior to this, he worked in the Pastoral Planning department of the Roman Catholic Diocese of Rochester as the coordinator of the parish visitation program. Richard began working for the church in 1996, after retiring from a 20-year career in law enforcement. He has also served as pastoral associate for the Church of the Nativity of the Blessed Virgin Mary in Brockport, NY, as campus minister for the State University of New York at Brockport, was the director of pastoral care for the Roman Catholic Community of the 19th Ward (a three parish cluster of churches) in the City of Rochester and worked in the Diocesan Tribunal for several years.

Dr. McCorry received his bachelors degree in 1992 from St. John Fisher College majoring in philosophy and religious studies and was inducted into Alpha Sigma Lambda, the National Continuing Education Honor Society. In 1998, he obtained his Master of Divinity degree from St. Bernard's School of Theology and Ministry. He also earned a Master of Science degree in organizational management from Roberts Wesleyan College in 1999 and received the Christian Service Award upon graduation. In 2004, he obtained a Doctor of Ministry degree, specializing in transformative leadership, from Colgate Rochester Crozer Divinity School.

Since 2001, he has led numerous workshops and reflection sessions throughout the Roman Catholic Diocese of Rochester on the topic of spirituality during times of change. These sessions are highly recommended by the Rochester Diocese as preparation for all those involved in pastoral planning. Dr. McCorry is the founder of **Embracing Change: A Spiritual Approach,** a change management consulting firm for dioceses and churches. For further information, you may consult his web site at: www.embracing-change.com.

0-595-31462-7